Balinese
Gardens

Balinese Gardens

Photographs by Luca Invernizzi Tettoni
Text by William Warren

With contributions by Tony Whitten,
Martin Jenkins and Adrian Vickers

PERIPLUS

Distributors

Indonesia
PT Java Books Indonesia, Jl Kelapa Gading Kirana,
Blok A14 No 17, Jakarta 14240.
Tel (62) 021 451 5351; Fax (62) 021 453 4987
Email: cs@javabooks.co.id

North America, Latin America & Europe
Tuttle Publishing, Airport Industrial Park,
364 Innovation Drive,
North Clarendon, VT 05759-9436.
Tel (802) 773 8930; Fax (802) 773 6993
Email: info@tuttlepublishing.com

Asia Pacific
Berkeley Books Pte Ltd,
130 Joo Seng Road, #06-01/03, Singapore 368357.
Tel (65) 6280 3320; Fax (65) 6280 6290
Email: inquiries@periplus.com.sg

Japan
Tuttle Publishing, Yaekari Building, 3rd Floor,
5-4-12 Osaki, Shinagawa-ku, Tokyo 141-0032.
Tel (03) 5437 0171; Fax (03) 5437 0755
Email: tuttle-sales@gol.com

Acknowledgments

The publisher would like to thank the management of Amanusa Resort, Bali Hyatt, Begawan Giri Estate, Four Seasons Resort Bali at Sayan and Jimbaran Bay, Grand Hyatt Bali and Novotel Benoa for permitting extensive coverage of their landmark gardens. Particular thanks are due to Julia Gajcak, Mark Hediger, Indrawati, Alistair McCracken, Kim Pawley, Royal Rowe, Peter Stettler and Ayun Sundari. Others who generously shared their gardens and their time include Lorne Blair; Bruce Carpenter; Jean-François Fichot; Gianni Francione; Bradley and Debora Gardner; Linda Garland; Rai Girigunadhi; Rodolfo Giusti; Rio Helmi; Brent Hesslyn; Philip Lakeman; R. A. Leonardi; Leonard Lueras; Milo Migliavacca; Didier Millet; Yohanes Minarwan; Graham Oldroyd; Cokorda Gde Ngurah Payangan; Carlo Pessina; Cody and Lyn Shwaiko; Martin Smith; Ir. A. A. Ngurah Mayun Udani; Marisa Viravaidhya; Wiya, Tatie and Agus Wawo-Runtu; Ian Van Werringan and Made Wijaya. Thanks also to Ida Bagus Sudibya. Adrian Vickers would like to thank Linda Connor and acknowledge his debt to the writings of Diana Darling, Mark Hobart, Christian Hooykaas and S. Supomo.

In memoriam to Lorne Blair, who passed away while the first edition of this book was in final production, the photographer and publisher would like to extend their heartfelt condolences to his family. We all miss him greatly.

Page 1: The Nikko Bali Resort at Nusa Dua features a stunning landscaped garden atop a cliff overlooking the sea.

Pages 2-3: The front courtyard at the home of two Australian artists in Ubud. Agave and Spanish Bayonet (*Yucca aoilfolia*) are set in a bed of decorative stones.

Published by Periplus Editions (HK) Ltd.

Copyright © 1995 Periplus Editions .
First paperback edition © 2004 Periplus Editions

Address all enquiries and comments to:
Periplus editorial office at
130 Joo Seng Road, #06-01/03, Singapore 368357

10 09 08 07 06 05 04
8 7 6 5 4 3 2 1

Contents

Gardens of Eden

"The morning of the world" was how Prime Minister Jawaharlal Nehru of India described Bali when he came as an official guest in the 1950s. To an earlier visitor, the American Hickman Powell, it was "the last paradise"; to others, a tropical Shangri–La, a refuge from worldly confusion, the very embodiment of a thousand tempting fantasies.

Bali has long exerted this peculiar power to seduce and stir the romantic imagination, not only among travellers fortunate enough to have beheld its charms with their own eyes, but also among a far greater number whose dreams derived from little more than its magically evocative name or through faded pictures in old *National Geographic* magazines. An important part of the allure, both in the past and today, is the island's omnipresent creativity and the richly complex culture of its people. "Everybody in Bali seems to be an artist," commented the painter Miguel Covarrubias. Another part of the appeal, equally strong, arises from the sheer physical beauty of the place.

"It takes a little time," as a newcomer to the tropics once wrote, "for the temperate mind to accept the palm–tree as a common, natural, and inevitable object in every outlook and landscape." A similar sense of botanical revelation occurs on any drive through Bali away from its few large towns. Along the coasts, coconut palms by the thousands form a permanent skyline of graceful fronds stirring in languid sea breezes, while elsewhere, huge Ficus trees wrap their roots around mossy walls, wild–looking jungles spill dramatically down picturesque ravines to streams and rivers, and tree ferns rise elegantly beside cool, shimmering lakes that adorn the craters of ancient volcanoes. In more settled places, a glimpse through the gateway of even the smallest courtyard reveals a riot of flowering shrubs and creepers, seemingly growing at random and clearly without much effort. There is a feeling of space, of Eden–like abundance, of moving through a vast but interconnected garden where every conceivable variation of green is on permanent display, from palest lime to purest emerald, accented here and there with a startling burst of colour.

Previous page: *The gardens of the Balina Serai hotel were planted in a coconut grove. All the existing trees were left in situ.*
Right: *Crinums, golden-flowered Allamanda, Plumeria and Caesalpinia in a garden created by Bradley Gardner at Begawan Giri Estate, near Ubud.*

Above: *Hemerocallis and a decorative fountain in front of the Eka Karya Botanic Gardens guest house at Bedugul, where the elevation encourages temperate climate plants to bloom.*

It thus comes as something of a surprise to discover that Bali is not only relatively small—a mere 144 kilometres at its widest and just 80 kilometres long—but is also one of the most densely populated places in the world: at is believed that as of the year 2000, Bali is supporting more than three million people.

There are several reasons why Bali's visual impact remains so powerful despite the stark reality of its statistics. It is blessed with fertile volcanic soil, ample water in the form of rain and natural springs, and equatorial temperatures that are, nearly everywhere, conducive to continual growth. The famous Wallace Line that divides the lush vegetation of subtropical Asia from the comparatively arid conditions of Australia runs along the narrow strait that separates Bali from Lombok, its closest neighbour.

Above: *The traditional gateway with Hemerocallis and Cannas in front of the Bali Handara Country Club; set inside an ancient volcanic crater, this is one of the most beautiful golf courses in the world. The large orange-floweringtree in the background is* Spathodea campanulata, *originally from West Africa.*

Moreover, although many parts of the island are intensely cultivated and have been for over 1000 years, the man–made aspects have a way of merging with its natural contours. Margaret Mead, the famous anthropologist, was struck by the constantly changing beauty of the rice fields, even in the more populated regions. Writing to a friend in 1936 from her base in Ubud, she noted "half a dozen characteristic but different aspects–those which are almost on a level, whose principal charm is the great variation in the same texture and colour as one small plot ripens an hour or a day behind the other, but all the varying shades remain within the same narrow range, and the flooded fields, which actually do mirror the sky, and the steep terraces, where the roots of each stalk stand out like sharp patterns along the edge."

There is yet another important factor–the deeply ingrained Balinese reverence for nature, which makes itself felt in countless ways. Trees, especially large ones like the *Waringin*, or Banyan, are looked upon as the abodes of spirits and are often the original reason for building a temple or shrine in a particular place. In villages, they provide a broad canopy for shows and dances held in the communal square. Flowers, too, play a cultural role; everywhere one sees the pristine white Plumeria, the bold Hibiscus, the papery bracts of Bougainvillea, the powerfully-scented *Michaelia champaca*, and numerous others, as offerings, incorporated into paintings, and woven into the glossy black hair of girls.

Bali's luxuriance is futher enhanced by more contemporary contributions to the landscape, a process that still continues. Many of the private homes and housing estates have gardens of singular beauty and horticultural richness, as do major resort hotels and even smaller guest bungalows. Nusa Dua, not many years ago a comparatively barren area near the island's southern tip, has been transformed through government initiative into a spacious park of green lawns, flowering trees and water features.

Like all islands born of volcanic violence, Bali acquired its rich variety of plants from the outside world only gradually over the millenia. The great majority of the ornamental trees and shrubs, as well as some of the others grown for commercial purposes, came to the island relatively recently. Many were brought by the Dutch during the 20th century from the great botanical gardens at Bogor, which in turn amassed a collection of plants from all over the tropical world. Still others arrived much more recently, introduced by private fanciers as exotic specimens for gardens or by landscape designers for their planting schemes at famous resort hotels.

Thriving in the rich earth, nurtured by the warm rains, these soon escaped their original confines and multiplied freely, often becoming almost wild. Who today would guess that Plumeria originated in the New World, *Delonix regia* in Madagascar, the Hibiscus in China, the Bougainvillea in Brazil? That the dazzling Red Gingers and Heliconias were comparatively rare only a few decades ago? All have become a part of Bali's natural scenery, in many cases part of its culture, adding their charms to a magical allure that remains as powerful as ever.

Above and Opposite (below): *Girls pause by a bridge near the aerial roots of the revered Banyan or Waringin tree.*

Opposite (top): *A quiet pathway leading to the garden restaurant at the Bali Hyatt in Sanur.*

Top: *The scarlet blooms of the Delonix regia, with its long seed pods, make a vivid contrast with a tropical sky.*

Above: *The white Plumeria is the most fragrant of the species, although pink and red flowered species, such as the one seen here, add a particular beauty to any garden.*

Left: *The gardens of Four Seasons Resort Bali at Jimbaran Bay, designed by Made Wijaya and begun in 1992. Wijaya says of the landscaping: "It was inspired by the backyard plantings in the neighbouring village of Pacatu–tight clumps of frangipani (Plumeria obtusa), pandanus and cactus trees. The seven village clusters, in contrast to the more artfully natural public areas, are 'done up' in Balinese village lane style with lots of poetic corners. The water features were essential–to cool the often baking hot site–and to provide an element of grandeur to the tight-packed main dining room pavilions."*

The Balinese Landscape

The island of Bali emerged from the seas in a series of cataclysmic volcanic explosions two to three million years ago—just the blink of an eye in geological time—and has been in the process of growing and changing ever since. A relatively minor eruption of Mount Agung in 1963, for example, blew out one billion cubic metres of matter, blasting away the top 130 metres of the volcano in the process, and depositing lava and ash over many parts of the island. Periodic explosions such as this one can literally change Bali's landscapes almost overnight.

Thanks largely to its turbulent origins and relative youth, Bali manages to cram an astonishing range of landforms into a fairly tiny area of just 5,500 square kilometres. The most obvious feature of the landscape is the sinuous backbone of volcanoes which runs the length of the island from east to west. Two other major regions, the lowland plains and limestone fringes, each play a vital role in Bali's unique topography.

Young Mountains and Ancient Reefs

Bali's volcanoes are dominated by Gunung (Mount) Agung in the east, which at 3,014 metres is still by far the tallest peak on the island, despite its recent dramatic shortening. West of this, the adjacent peaks of Mount Batur and Mount Abang are 1,000 metres shorter than Agung.

Along the northeastern flanks of Agung, around the diving spot of Tulamben, spectacular lava flows from the 1963 eruption spill into the ocean, forming the most recent addition to Bali's landscape. The stark scrub vegetation found growing over the dark lava here give an indication of what the entire island may have looked like when it first emerged from the sea.

Mount Batur, at the centre of the island, nestles dramatically in the midst of one of the world's largest calderas beside a huge crater lake. Tongues of lava fan out from the central cone of the volcano, many of them resulting from different eruptions at very different times. The more recent flows are still black and unvegetated even after several decades of exposure to the elements, while the earlier ones are already brown and overgrown.

Left: This scene at Bukit Jambul typifies Bali at its most fertile, with plantations of clove trees (seen to the left) and coconut palms interspersed by terraced rice fields.

Opposite: The Ayung River, Bali's largest, cuts through soft volanic rock to form a ravine so typical of the terrain around Bali's central volcanoes.
Above: Nestling part way down a ravine, a farmer's house is surrounded by fruit trees.

The outer slopes of the massive Batur caldera, which form much of central Bali, are scored by deep ravines with precipitous sides that have been cut by rivers running through the soft tuff rock, a common feature throughout the island. Continuing to the west, the mountains separating Lovina from Negara are also of volcanic origin, but date from a much earlier era, so their craters have long since disappeared; the only sign of their volcanic origins is a few sulfurous springs which dot the region.

North and south of Bali's volcanic backbone lie the coastal plains which form Bali's rice bowl. Most of Bali's lowlands, and certainly all the fertile parts, have been formed by deposits from numerous volcanic eruptions. Along the coasts fringing the lowlands are black sand beaches consisting of fine volcanic particles. By contrast, other beaches such as the one at Sanur, are lighter in colour and composed of rough volcanic and coral particles mixed with the shells of countless billions of marine organisms.

Several parts of Bali meanwhile are non-volcanic and stand in sharp contrast to the rest of the island. These are the limestone (fossil coral reef) areas of the southern fringe, chiefly at Negara in the west and on the Bukit Peninsula south of the airport, where the luxury hotels of Nusa Dua are located. Like many limestone regions, these areas have poor soils and are difficult to cultivate.

The Human Side of Bali's Landscape

For all the rugged natural beauty of many of the wilder parts of Bali–the volcanoes and lakes, lava fields, forests and seashore cliffs–the overwhelming impression is of a profoundly humanised landscape. People probably first arrived on Bali between three and four thousand years ago and have been moulding the island to meet their needs ever since.

The most striking manifestation of this is the intricate patchwork of innumerable rice fields which covers many parts of the lowlands and climbs the hills and lower slopes of the mountains in tier after tier, creating one of the most harmonious and beautiful meldings of the natural and the man-made on earth. Bali's rice fields represent one of the most sophisticated and stable examples anywhere of a traditional agricultural system, a system which has been in place for nigh on a thousand years and which has much to teach modern-day farmers elsewhere.

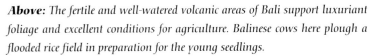

Above: *The fertile and well-watered volcanic areas of Bali support luxuriant foliage and excellent conditions for agriculture. Balinese cows here plough a flooded rice field in preparation for the young seedlings.*

Above Right: *Water is considered to be sacred in Bali. A bamboo conduit carries water here from a sacred spring; it is then collected to be used as holy water in temple ceremonies.*

Rice is more than just a staple food for the Balinese; it is a cultural and spiritual lynchpin whose cultivation has had a profound influence on the structure of Balinese society. It is even personified as a deity, the goddess Bhatari Sri. The commonest form of rice cultivation on Bali is the wetland or *sawah* system of flooded fields, where the water is retained by low banks or bunds. Most *sawah* fields may be watered by irrigation; the seasonal nature of the rainfall on Bali, especially at lower altitudes where the rice is grown, means that a scant one per cent of the 100,000 hectares or so of *sawah* is rain fed.

Almost 20 per cent of Bali's land is devoted to another traditional form of cultivation–the *kebun* or home garden. These are an intricate, mixed-cultivation system in which as many as 50 different crops of all shapes and sizes may be grown. The tallest trees are generally durians or coconuts, below which grow other fruit trees such as *rambutan*, jackfruit and mango, providing a lush, dark-green canopy. Also important are the nutritious papaya and the ubiquitous banana, grown not only for its fruit and edible stem but for its leaves, which have a thousand and one uses. Interplanted with these are tall ground crops such as maize and cassava, while nearer the soil are other vegetables such as taro, various spices and scrambling sweet potatoes. There are also climbers such as yam, passionfruit and melons, which can reach up into the tops of the tallest trees.

The *kebun* helps to ensure that Balinese families can enjoy a varied and nutritious diet, for at any given time of year, a wide

Left: *The emerald-coloured grass growing up the walls of the rice terraces contrasts with the ripening heads of rice.*

Below: *Variations in colour from green to gold reflect the different stages of plantings of the all-important rice; a surprising 99 per cent of Bali's rice crop is grown in irrigated fields.*

range of crops will be ready for harvest. It is not, however, just a kitchen garden, for the system is increasingly used to provide crops for sale within Bali and for export. Notable amongst these are coffee, cloves, vanilla and even the Hydrangea flowers which are used in Balinese votive offerings, all of which flourish in the shade of the larger trees in the *kebun*.

The *sawah* and *kebun* apart, one of the most distinctive features of the Balinese landscape are the enormous fig or *Waringin* trees which grow along the roads, close to or in temples. These magnificent trees are extremely important to fruit-eating birds and insects since they bear numerous small sweetish fruits.

Wild Rivers and Mountain Lakes

With its mountainous topography and heavy seasonal rainfall, it is not surprising that Bali has more than its fair share of rivers and streams. What is surprising, for such an apparently lush island, is that only about half of Bali's 162 named rivers and streams flow year round; the rest hold water only during the rainy season, normally from November to April.

The heavy monsoon rains create a powerful flow of water which cuts easily through the soft volcanic rocks; thus, most of Bali's rivers and streams flow in the bottom of deep, steep-sided valleys or ravines until they reach the coastal lowlands. Most rivers are short, flowing for less than 30 kilometres.

Bali's lowlands are singularly devoid of natural lakes. However, several are found in the central part of the highlands. By far the

Opposite: *Lying within a vast caldera at the island's centre, Batur is Bali's biggest lake and the source of an underground network of water channels which feed into sacred springs all up and down the slopes of Mount Batur.*
Left: *The landmark temple, Pura Ulun Danu Bratan, dedicated to the goddess of Lake Bratan, lies within another volcanic crater to the west of Batur.*
Below: *Lake Tamblingan and Lake Buyan, seen to the far left, are thought to have once been a single lake which was later split in two by a lava flow.*

Top: The white sand beach at Nusa Dua, with the towering cone of Gunung Agung visible in the background.

Above: The spectacular cliffs on the west side of the Bukit Peninsula, near the famous Ulu Watu temple; the shoreline in the distance is East Java.

Right: The dramatic black sand beach at Kusamba, like many around the island, is composed of volcanic particles spewed out from Mount Agung, a still-active volcano. In the background is the island of Nusa Penida.

largest, most spectacular and most important to the Balinese is Lake Batur, covering just over 1,700 hectares in the ancient caldera surrounding Mount Batur. Some 30 kilometres to the west of Lake Batur are three much smaller but still impressive crater lakes at similar altitude: Lake Bratan, Lake Buyan and Lake Tamblingan. These were probably once a single lake before lava flowed across it, isolating one body of water from the next. Tamblingan is the least disturbed, most beautiful and most remote lake, while Bratan and Buyan have extensive areas of market gardens around their shores.

Fertile Bounty of Bali's Volcanoes

The soft volcanic rock and ash of the mountains are easily weathered and broken down to make a thick layer of finely textured topsoil which is generally rich in minerals and extremely fertile. In addition, the topsoil is very well drained, ensuring that there is little risk of flooding; yet it is also highly prone to leaching, as the rain easily washes out minerals. The soils at higher altitudes are particularly susceptible to this, as their only source of water is from the atmosphere. Soils lower down benefit from the loss of those further up, as they are enriched by minerals carried down in streams and irrigation water. Counterbalancing this, the soils at higher altitudes tend to be younger and thereby intrinsically more mineral–rich and fertile than those lower down. The older, low–lying soils have gradually lost their minerals over the years, resulting in an acid, kaolin–rich clay.

Leaching is most marked in wetter areas. In seasonally dry regions, evaporation from the soil tends to pull dissolved minerals up through the soil, thereby maintaining fertility. However, clay soils are sticky and hard to work when wet, as hard as concrete and cracked when dry. Thus, plants and farmers in different parts of Bali are faced with opposing problems: either there is adequate rainfall and a constant battle to maintain fertility, or reasonable fertility but highly seasonal rainfall and difficult soils. However, the clayey quality of much of the soil allows the construction of stable terraces on precipitous slopes which, in many other parts of the world, would pose a severe threat of erosion. The terraced bunds made of Bali's sunbaked clay can be almost as hard and stable as brickwork although they nevertheless require a good deal of maintenance.

Above and Right: *Bali's rice fields, watered by a thousand-year-old irrigation system, occupy fertile lowlands and volcanic hillsides alike.*

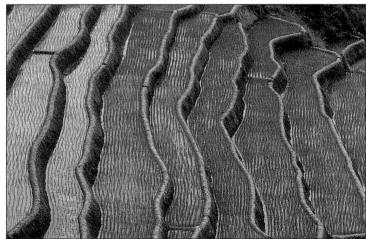

Below and Bottom: The relatively dry land along the northeast coast near Tulamben, was covered in lava flows by the eruption of Mount Agung in 1963, and thus exhibits a very different vegetation from the rest of the island.

Seasons in the Sun

Bali's volcanoes provide the raw material of which the island is composed. However, climate determines to a large extent which plants can grow on these soils. Lying within the moist tropics, Bali seems to visitors to be almost unfairly blessed, with abundant but not excessive rainfall and warm but not overly hot temperatures year round. The true picture is more complex. Despite its equatorial position, Bali's climate is markedly seasonal and shows notable variations from year to year. Moreover, the island's varied topography leads to great regional variations, some areas being much cooler and others more arid than one might expect.

From November to March, Bali has hot and wet weather. The rest of the year is cooler and drier, as the island is influenced by the dry southeast monsoon winds which blow in from the Australian continent during the middle of the year.

Bali thus has three major climate zones: the wet mountains, which receive over 300 centimetres of rain a year and where mosses and lichens adorn the stone of temples and shrines and the vegetation is lush; the lowlands and hills, where the average annual rainfall is about 200 centimetres, most of it falling in the four or five months around Christmas, and the very dry fringe areas at the northern, southern and western edges of the island. Temperatures change with altitude much more than with the seasons, and ground frosts may occur under clear night skies in hollows above 1,500 metres. Lowland daytime temperatures vary little between the dry and rainy seasons, from 28°–29°C to 30°–31°C respectively.

A Thousand-Year-Old System

The farmers of Bali organise their *sawah* irrigation through *subaks*, which are autonomous cooperatives of rice farmers who are all dependent on the same water supply. *Subaks* are socio–religious groupings which are organised through a hierarchical system of water temples, linked ultimately to the great temple of Ulun Lake Batur, the temple of the lake below Mount Batur, traditionally regarded as the source of all irrigation water on Bali. The arrangement of *subaks* is determined by local drainage and water-flow patterns, so that one village may have members of several different *subaks* within it. They are responsible for the maintenance of the system of irrigation channels, tunnels and

Above: *The procession just seen wending its way through the rice fields is on the way to collect holy water from a spring on Mount Agung.*

Opposite: *Vegetation scales right up the flanks of Bali's sacred mountain, Gunung Agung, a volcano that erupted with devastating results in 1963. The outpouring of ash helps fertilise rice fields such as these, which seem to resemble an amphitheatre.*

weirs, as well as the instigation of fallow periods and the determination of rice–planting times.

The influence and importance of the *subak* system was greatly underestimated by the Dutch colonial authorities, an attitude which persisted in the post-colonial era, until a few years ago. For example, the role that coordination of rice–planting times over a wide area plays in the control of certain pests was not appreciated by outsiders until very recently, although it was obviously well understood by the local people for centuries.

Even under optimum conditions, only two rice crops a year are practicable in any one field. To maximise the use of arable land on this densely populated island, dryland crops such as maize, cassava, sweet potatoes, groundnuts and soya beans are grown as part of the rotation under non–flooded conditions after the rice has been harvested.

On Bali, practically every square metre of arable land within reach of a source of irrigation water is under *sawah* cultivation. Rather surprisingly, this accounts for only around 20 per cent of the island, concentrated in the southern lowlands and in the region of the north around Singaraja. Rather more than this–just under one–third of the island–is given over to non–irrigated or dryland fields which produce just one rain-fed crop each year.

The distribution of arable land and access to irrigation water have had a profound effect on human settlement patterns in Bali. This is perhaps best illustrated by looking at the arrangement of the traditional nine kingdoms into which Bali was divided. Seven of these are concentrated in the fertile region to the south or southwest of Mount Agung and Mount Batur. The drier, narrower north coast and the west, with its extensive areas of infertile limestone, could only support one kingdom apiece.

In modern times, particularly the last two or three decades, there have been profound and far–reaching changes in the distribution of population. The growth of tourism and the beginnings of industrialisation have drawn increasing numbers of people to certain areas, especially along the coast, which formerly supported much lower populations. Land, some of it once productive, is continually being lost to urbanisation. This, along with the ever-growing population, is placing increasing pressure on Bali's fertile soils and traditional agricultural systems.

Plants of Bali

The great Victorian naturalist, A.R. Wallace, who visited these islands in the mid–19th century, noted that there was something special about the position of Bali. Looking at the island's animal life, and comparing it with that of neighboring areas, he observed a startling difference between the faunal composition of Bali and the island of Lombok just to the east, despite the fact that the two are separated only by a narrow strait 40 kilometres wide. Wallace therefore concluded that this strait marks a division between two of the world's great biogeographic realms, the Asian and the Australian. He tracked this dividing line, which came to be known as Wallace's Line, farther northwards between Borneo and Sulawesi, and thence to the strait separating Sulawesi from the Philippines.

As it turns out, Wallace's Line traces the edge of the huge Sunda continental shelf, which has Bali as its southeastern outpost. Much of the Sunda shelf is now submerged under the South China Sea, but at several periods in the past it was exposed and what are now the islands of Sumatra, Java, Borneo and Bali were connected to the Asian mainland by land bridges.

Bali's flora, therefore, has far stronger connections with the west than the east; it is effectively a reduced version of Java's flora, which is itself poorer in species than the islands of Borneo and Sumatra. "Impoverished" is, however, a relative term, for there are at least 4,500 native plant species found on Bali.

Bali's Shrinking Forests

So pervasive has mankind's influence been on the landscape of Bali in the last 4,000 years that it is extremely difficult to determine what the vegetation of the island looked like before man's arrival. When the island first emerged from the seas, it found itself in a biologically rich region of tropical forest flora, a ready source of vegetation for the newly emerged volcanic landscape.

It seems that at the end of the last ice age around 8,000 years ago, Bali was covered in various forms of forest, both evergreen and deciduous, although vegetation high on the volcanoes above the tree line was very limited in extent. Ecologists have classified

Left: The cooler climate of the highlands above Lake Bratan encourages the growth of Dicksonia sp., although the showy Spathodea campanulata (in the background) more commonly seen in the lowlands still flourishes here.

Above: *Bali's mangrove forests are now reduced to about five square kilometres; this patch is south of the airport, flanking the road to Nusa Dua.*

Above Right: *This hardy, salt-resistant plant is one of the several types of Pandanus (screwpine) which thrive along Bali's beaches.*

Right: *Staghorn Ferns (Platycerium coronarium) grow wild on tree trunks and branches.*

Opposite: *The intense crowding of vegetation in a patch of rainforest completely obscures the soil; even the trees are covered with mosses, Bird's Nest Ferns (Asplenium nidus) and other creepers.*

Opposite Right: *A close-up view of ferns in the rainforest.*

Bali's forests into six major types, although in practice it is impossible to actually see where one type begins and another ends. The types of forest are: evergreen rain forest, semi-evergreen rain forest, moist deciduous forest, dry deciduous forest, seasonal montane forest and aseasonal montane forest.

Moist deciduous or monsoonal forest was originally the most common form of vegetation, covering an estimated 43% of the island, including most of the central uplands. This is scarcely surprising, given the wet but highly seasonal nature of Bali's climate. The moist deciduous forest, along with virtually all other forest types on Bali, has been drastically reduced in extent.

Straddling the border between the land and the sea are mangrove forests, mainly growing in tidal flats around Benoa Bay. Many have now been reclaimed and only around 5 square km of mangrove forest still exist on Bali; it is quite likely that they were never very extensive. Bali's sandy beaches are dominated by the purple-flowered Morning Glory (*Ipomoea pescaprae*) along with other creeping plants which help to stabilise the sand. In some areas, the shoreline forests are dominated by *Barringtonia asiatica* and Screwpine (*Pandanus tectorius*), Yellow Beach Hibiscus (*Hibiscus tiliaceus*), Cycads (*Cycas rumphii*) and other salt-tolerant species.

Lowland forests were formerly common in most inland areas. The limestone forests of the southern coasts are almost entirely cleared or degraded, and most of the area is now scrub dominated by introduced plants such as *Lantana* and the composite *Chromolaena* (formerly known as *Eupatorium*).

Top: Vanda tricolor, *a fragrant orchid still found growing wild in some parts of Bali, is also cultivated in gardens around the island.*
Above: *Young buds of the clove tree, which are picked in an immature state and then dried before being used as a spice.*

In the east and northwest are deciduous forests, growing in conditions varying from moist to very dry. These are highly susceptible to fire during the dry season and have been modified wherever they are found. In the northwest is open savannah forest dominated by flat-topped crowns of spreading Acacia trees and huge, smooth-trunked Borassus palms. On the Prapat Agung Peninsula at the western tip of the island, inside the Bali Barat National Park, is found one of the most unusual forests in Bali, a single-species stand of *Sawo kecik* trees (*Manilkara kauki*) whose rounded grey crowns can be seen from the Java–Bali ferry, giving the impression of a temperate woodland rather than a tropical forest. The lowland rain forest meanwhile has been almost entirely destroyed, although some of the deep, steep and inaccessible river-cut ravines have remnants of it clinging to their sides.

The transition to montane forest begins around 1,500 metres. One of the most striking aspects of this for visitors from temperate regions is the increasing number of familiar-looking plants. The upper montane forest is characterised by species of Rhododendron, Bilberries and Wintergreen, with Gentians, Honeysuckles, Primulas, Buttercups and Asters all found in abundance.

Edelweiss and Other Rarities

The richness of Bali's remaining areas of natural vegetation can be somewhat overwhelming initially; nevertheless, there are some plants which definitely merit closer inspection. In the mountain regions, the most renowned plant is undoubtedly the Javan Edelweiss, *Anaphalis javanica*. This giant member of the daisy family has white-furred leaves, stems as thick as a human leg and is capable of reaching 8 metres in height. Its beauty and prominence in a region where few large plants can gain a foothold has proved rather to its detriment, as pieces are frequently picked by walkers, either as a souvenir or because the plant has spiritual or religious connotations; large plants are consequently now very rare.

Bali's relatively brief history and its proximity to Java mean that it has very few species that are truly unique to the island. However, endemics do exist, and include the white-flowered ground orchid, *Calanthe baliensis*, which is known only from forests behind the Eka Karya Botanical Garden at Candi Kuning, and a mistletoe, *Ameyema longipes*. This has been collected only three times, at altitudes of 1,600 to 1,935 metres. It was last recorded in

1936 and its rediscovery would be a great reward for a sharp-eyed botanist. Amongst the trees, there is an unnamed areca palm, in the genus *Pinanga*, with massive, single stems; this was discovered in montane forest near Bedugul in 1973 and has not been recorded elsewhere.

As well as these endemics, Bali has a number of species shared with Java but found nowhere else. Indeed, it is likely that several plants known only from Bali also occur, or rather once occurred, on Java. Amongst those still surviving on the two islands are another orchid, *Malleola baliensis*, a small but attractive epiphytic plant with a 9-cm inflorescence of yellow and white flowers, and a thorny leguminous tree, *Erythrina euodiphylla*, of the dry forest.

A tiny patch of largely artificial forest at Sangeh, an area famous for its Monkey Forest Temple, is the only known locality of the tree *Dipterocarpus hasseltii*. Most Southeast Asian rain forests consist of trees from the dipterocarp family; their winged seeds give rise to their name, which literally means "two-winged-fruits".

Nature's Strongholds

The ever increasing human population on Bali, and the ever growing number of visitors, is placing more and more pressure on the island's few remaining areas of natural habitat. Not only is this a serious menace to the surviving wild animal and plant species, some of them rare and localised, but it also threatens to undermine the agricultural systems which have served the island's human inhabitants so well for centuries.

To try to preserve what is left of Bali's nature, there are four small reserves. The best known is Bali Barat National Park. The decision to transform this forest and savannah area of 19,366 hectares into a game reserve was first reached by Bali's Council of Kings in 1947. The national park covers about the same area and its goal is to balance conservation and human needs. Some areas are a wilderness for wildlife, while areas on the perimeter near human habitation serve as buffer zones, providing villagers with forest resources but serving as a barrier to encroachment.

Bali's other reserves are but a fraction of the size of the national park. The largest, Gunung Batukau Nature Reserve, comprises three separate areas around volcanic lakes in the centre of the island. Their combined area is only 1,763 hectares and really should be extended to encompass all the remaining forest in the

Above: *The deciduous forest around Lake Bratan looks almost European, providing a marked contrast to the lush vegetation found in rain forest areas.*

Top Left: *The red-orange blooms of the African Tulip Tree.*

Top Right: *The Coral Tree (Erythrina spp.) is a member of the pea family.*

Above: *One of the many hybrid Hibiscus found in Bali.*

Above Right: *The furry* Bixa orellana *pods contain seeds used to colour food in South America and the Philippines.*

Right: *Delicate lavender flowers of the Thunbergia grandiflora.*

Far Right: *The popular and decorative Alpinia purpurata.*

Top Left: *The Pink Trumpet Tree or* Tabebuia rosea.

Top Right: Ipomaea horsfalliae, *a member of the Morning Glory family.*

Above: Clerodendron paniculatum *(the Pagoda flower), one of the few Southeast Asian natives found in contemporary Balinese gardens.*

Above Left: *White flowers of the fragrant Plumeria.*

Far Left: *The hanging Hibiscus schizopetalus.*

Left: *The common Hibiscus rosa–sinensis.*

Top: *The largest of all tropical fruits, the jackfruit* (Artocarpus hetero-phyllus) *can weigh as much as 50 kilos.*
Above: *Rambutan* (Nephelium lappaceum) *has a white, sweet interior.*
Opposite Top: *Thorny durians are the most highly prized fruit in Bali.*
Opposite Middle: *Golden coconuts grow on a dwarf variety of the familiar coconut palm; their decorative appearance makes them popular offerings.*
Opposite Below: *Breadfruit* (Artocarpus sp) *needs to be cooked before eating, and is a standard provider of starch in the Balinese diet.*
Overleaf: *Some of the useful plants of Bali include cloves (far right, bottom), the lontar palm (second from right, top), betel leaves (far right, centre) as well as varieties of bamboo and palm fruits. The salak fruit (second from left, bottom) is especially prized in Bali for its sour-sweetness and grows in the district of Sibetan in east Bali*

area, which would then cover an altitudinal range from 700 metres to 2,278 metres. There is easy access to the forest from the Eka Karya Botanical Gardens near Candi Kuning and from the Pura Luhur Batukau temple, from which an energetic walker can reach the summit of Mount Batukau in about four hours. There are some fine views, grand trees and interesting altitudinal changes in the vegetation along the way. East of here, the 540-hectare Penelokan Tourist Park sits astride the southern rim of Mount Batur, overlooking the famous Batur caldera lake. The scenery of this park is justifiably celebrated, but its contribution to nature conservation is rather less significant. Finally, there is the tiny, 10-hectare nature reserve at Sangeh, a traditional sacred forest with its own temple, complete with resident macaque monkeys. It is here that the population of *Dipterocarpus hasseltii* trees grows. It has been argued that this is the last remnant of true lowland rain forest on Bali, but it seems certain that the forest has been heavily altered by people and that a significant number of the trees were actually planted.

Some Roadside Tree Crops

The coconut (*Cocos nucifera*) is one of the most numerous trees in Bali and almost all parts of the coconut are used. Oil, used mainly for cooking and in soap, is extracted from the dried fruit flesh; the mature flesh is grated to extract coconut milk, the basis of so many Indonesian dishes. The hard shell is used to make utensils or charcoal, while the husk fibre or coir is used for ropes, mats and brushes. One of the most striking uses of the fronds is the plaiting and bending of young leaves into unique decorations.

Many northern hill slopes in central Bali are covered by dense groves of cone-shaped trees with lime-green leaves suffused with red. These are clove trees (*Syzygium aromaticum*), the young flower buds of which are picked and dried to make the well-known spice. About 85% of Indonesia's annual crop of nearly 30,000 tonnes is made into the distinctive clove-scented *kretek* cigarettes which assail the nasal nerves of visitors to Indonesia.

On the hills of Bali, particularly around the volcanic crater lakes, coffee trees of African origin are planted beneath taller fruit trees. They have clusters of jasmine-scented white flowers; the berries, which are dark red when ripe, contain a two-part "bean". dried prior to grinding and roasting.

Gardener's Delights

Bali's rich and varied forests have, over the years, proved a fertile hunting ground for collectors on the lookout for ornamental plants to be brought into cultivation. Of all the varied plant families whose members are grown in gardens and greenhouses around the world, none has such an exotic allure as the largest of all, the orchid family or Orchidaceae.

Although we generally think of orchids as spectacular, large-flowered plants, a large proportion of species are, in fact, small and inconspicuous with dull-coloured flowers. One of the wonderful exceptions is the dramatic and beautiful Moon Orchid (*Phalaenopsis amabilis*), Indonesia's national flower. With its metre-long inflorescence of pure white and yellow flowers, the Moon Orchid has been sadly depleted in the wild but is common in cultivation. Still commonly collected from the wild and offered for sale on roadsides and in markets is the beautiful *Vanda tricolor.* Fortunately, this Vanda is an adaptable plant and can still be seen growing wild in some less accessible parts of Bali.

Far less common than the Vanda is the only Lady's Slipper orchid which grows on Bali, *Paphiopedilum lowii*, one of the larger species of Paphiopedilum, with multiple scapes of pink, green and brown flowers. All plants of this Asian genus are in demand by collectors and many have been much depleted in the wild. *Paphiopedilum lowii* is one of the more widespread species and is less eagerly sought after than many of the others, but has still suffered at the hands of unscrupulous collectors. Export of wild-collected plants of this and other Paphiopedilum species is now illegal.

Several other Balinese orchids are in cultivation, but usually only grown by specialists. These include *Dendrobium spathilingue*, a sprawling species with scapes of very attractive, large, pink-suffused white flowers with a yellow throat and the smaller, more delicate *Dendrobium linearifolium*, one of the most light-tolerant of Bali's orchids, which can be seen growing in full sunlight.

Amongst other plant families present on Bali, the Gesneriads (Gesneriaceae) have provided several popular pot-plants, such as the trailing Lipstick Plant (*Aeschynanthus radicans*) with bright orange-red tubular flowers, often grown in hanging baskets in conservatories and greenhouses.

Traditional Gardens in Bali

Traditional Balinese gardens are generally quite spare, consisting of one or two trees and a lot of open space–packed earth swept bare–with a few flowers around. Often the trees are off to one side, sometimes in pots, and have staghorns growing on them, with perhaps one or two potted flowering plants added for decoration.

The guiding æsthetic principle of traditional Balinese gardens is a variation on the contrast between overcrowded abundance (*ramé*) and empty stillness (*sepi*). A few decades ago, most gardens on the island tended more towards the *sepi* side, in the style mentioned above, with perhaps the odd Croton or Coleus added for colour. In more recent years, the *ramé* end of the spectrum has come into favour, featuring a profusion of brightly–coloured plants.

Venerable Temple Trees

Banyan trees, called *Bingin* or *Waringin* in Balinese, old trees with multiple trunks and aerial roots hanging down, are important landmarks at certain well–defined places in Bali. They grow at major crossroads and in front of important village temples. And no traditional palace should be without one in its forecourt. It is believed that they are a favourite haunt of invisible spirits.

Many other trees found in or next to temples share in the potency of site which caused a temple to be built there in the first place. Stories of the founding of temples often have it that the invisible forces around a particular tree lead to the establishment of a temple in which offerings are made to them.

In a number of legends from Bali and elsewhere in Indonesia, the *Nagasari* (*Mesua ferrea*) tree is linked to temples and to the divine. Ancient Javanese temples in particular have these beautiful trees growing abundantly. Another tree with temple associations is the huge *Kepuh* (*Sterculia foetida*), whose bare limbs and desolate appearance make it particularly suited to graveyards and temples associated with death and the fearsome goddess Durga, the context in which most Balinese place this tree. In paintings and in the *wayang kulit* shadow theatre, the *Kepuh* is shown hung with entrails and scores of carrion birds perching on its limbs.

Left: *Tirta Gangga (literally "Ganges Water"), the opulent pleasure garden of the kings of Karangasem in eastern Bali, who were the foremost Balinese garden builders of the 19th and early 20th centuries.*

Above: *A* Kepuh *tree* (Sterculia foetida): *in the* wayang kulit *shadow theatre, it has its own special puppet. Its desolate appearance makes it particularly suited to planting in graveyards and temples associated with death.*
Above Middle: *The* Waringin *or* Banyan *tree, a glorious, powerful tree that can be seen for miles away, has mystical associations in Balinese culture.*
Above Right: *The pretty white flowers of the* Mesua ferrea, *also known as the Ceylon Ironwood.*

Garden Temples

The most famous temple garden in Bali is Pura Taman Ayun, part of the former capital of the kingdom of Mengwi, sited just to the east of the royal palace. Its garden (*taman*) aspect is mainly indicated by the fact that it is surrounded by a moat. This is of course true of most other royal garden temples, which have few trees growing in them, but whose ponds or canals represent the oceans of the Hindu cosmos, and thus convey on them a special status.

The house shrine of the palace of Kesiman is another example of this garden temple design, with its special pond and giant *kulkul* tower. These gardens all represent pleasure, but pleasure which unites the divine forces and the royal ancestors who are commemorated in such temples. The intermediaries in this communion are the divine nymphs who are associated with all such gardens and bathing places. And the association is furthered by the presence of sacred pink and white lotus flowers floating in the ponds, where nymphs and deities like to take their rest.

Palace Gardens: The Royal Prerogative

Before the Dutch conquest of Bali, only kings had gardens. They were constructed along the same basic lines as garden temples, consisting of pavilions with ponds in or around them, and a few trees. Fountains and water spouts carved in the form of snakes, elephants or demons were common features. In some old texts there are descriptions of "forest gardens" which were small forests situated inside palaces, again with cosmological significance.

Left: *Pura Taman Ayun, reputed to have been designed by a Chinese architect, is surrounded by a moat and echoes the Hindu-Balinese interpretation of the cosmos in its layout.*

Below: *Pura Pelet in Mengwi, with its well maintained garden. A Mussaenda, with striking pink bracts, can be seen to the right, while day-blooming white water lilies fill the pond.*

Above: *The imposing gateway leading to the private family quarters of the palace at Ubud; dance performances are regularly held in the palace forecourt, with this gateway as the backdrop.*

Right: *This floating pavilion is an integral part of the 17th-century Western Palace, built by the rulers of Karangasem.*

Below: Entrance to the Puri Gede of Karambitan, one of three traditional palaces found in this small village in Tabanan district.

The Layout of Palaces

Balinese kings and princes built their palaces in accordance with classical Hindu–Javanese models, striving to imitate the capitals of the great Javanese kingdoms of old. They were supposed to model the cosmos on a miniature scale and consisted of a number of walled compounds joined together. There were sleeping compounds for the king and his second ruler (usually the crown prince or the king's brother), the main wives, the secondary wives, the concubines and the servants. There were also food preparation areas, rice barns, the treasury and the arsenal.

The gardens were walled portions of natural foliage that served a rather special function in the classical Balinese–Javanese tradition, symbolically joining the sacred mountain, symbolised by pointed temple shrines or peaked roofs of the palace pavilions, with the sea, symbolised by moats and ponds. In other words, the *taman* represented the world that lay between these two extremes.

A feature common to all palaces was the forecourt, called the *bañcingah*, where the king held audience with commoners and where special pavilions were set aside for theatrical performances of *gambuh* dance–drama. At the rear of this courtyard, rising over the whole palace, was a great gate marking the space beyond which ordinary subjects could not enter. Beyond the forecourt was a ceremonial courtyard, and near it was an important shrine dedicated to the royal ancestors, which usually had an offering area in front of it.

The only other people who were allowed to have formal gardens were priests. Their houses, called *geria*, had gardens which were designed for meditation; some were even called *geria taman*. Most have collections of plants which are placed there for their decorative flowers, perhaps closer to the Western idea of a private garden than the royal ponds.

The "Floating Pavilion" at Klungkung

Bali's greatest palace gardens almost invariably featured a *balé kambang* or "floating pavilion", an artificial island with a pavilion standing on it, surrounded by a moat or artificial lake. The best remaining example stands in the former palace of the kings of Klungkung. It was largely devastated in 1908 when the royal family marched to their deaths in ritual suicide against the guns

Above: The imposing gate at the entrance to the former palace of Klungkung, now a museum and one of the most popular tourist sites in Bali.

Opposite: The best example of a balé kambang or "floating pavilion" in Bali still stands in the palace of the former kings of Klungkung, Bali's oldest and most revered dynasty. Like all traditional Balinese pleasure gardens it is intended to model the Hindu cosmos, with a central pavilion representing the sacred Mount Meru surrounded by concentric continents and oceans.

of invading Dutch forces., but once extended 250 metres further to the south of the present pavilions, and in front of it was an open field planted with a single, massive Banyan tree. This tree has now been cut down.

The focal point of the pleasure garden of the Klungkung palace was the lotus pond with pavilion. The present pavilion standing in the pond is not the original one (this has been relocated and is used for ceremonies in the new palace, constructed nearby in the 1930s), but a larger replacement. In the 1940s, the new floating pavilion had its ceilings grandly painted by Wayan Kayun, the master artist from the nearby village of Kamasan.

The Denpasar Palace

The other palace which had a grand garden was the former *puri* of Denpasar, situated where the town square of Bali's capital is now located. This was also destroyed in a stand against the Dutch in 1906. Built at the beginning of the 19th century, this great palace featured a large garden area in the courtyard next to the forecourt. This courtyard had a huge building called the "Pavilion of Beauty" where the king slept. Another pavilion was set atop the palace wall, from which vantage point the king could watch his subjects. A central complex of four pleasure pavilions was entirely surrounded by water, the whole yard being called Narmada after the sacred river of India. The sleeping quarters of that king's principal wives adjoined this courtyard. There was also another small garden on the eastern side of the palace; featuring lotus ponds and a library, it was called Saraswati after the goddess of learning.

Gianyar and Karangasem

Two of the best-preserved traditional palaces in Bali, both still occupied and featuring pleasure gardens, are found in Gianyar and Karangasem (now called Amlapura). The Gianyar palace was rebuilt substantially in the 1890s after devastating internal wars split the kingdom, and features a garden with symbolic mountain shrine and an adjacent walled ritual area to the north. The old palace of the eastern Balinese kingdom of Karangasem was built in the 17th century, as the dynasty expanded to become the most powerful on Bali, even conquering the western parts of the neighbouring island of Lombok. Rulers of the Karangasem

Top: *The entrance to the Puri Gede at Karambitan, a fine example of traditional palace courtyard design.*

Above: *The living quarters of the Karambitan palaces reflects modern trends in Indonesian gardening, known as tamanisasi, with orderly rows of shrubs and neat pathways. The gardens of this and many Balinese homes have come to resemble a cross between Dutch colonial gardens and tourist bungalows.*

dynasty were Bali's foremost garden builders in the 19th and 20th centuries. The last king of the line expanded the Puri Kangin or Eastern Palace, and also expanded the bathing area at Tirta Gangga, which still exists.

The king's greatest achievement, however, was the splendid pleasure garden at Ujung, several kilometres south of the capital near the coast. Destroyed in the early 1980s by an earthquake, this garden consisted of sets of square ponds with central islands. The main pond had on its island, accessible by bridges, a large building built high above the water so as to cool its inhabitants with the afternoon breezes. Above all this stood a gazebo–like observation pavilion, while a variety of cosmological symbols set on the adjoining hills indicated how the garden was intended to represent the unity of all the elements of nature.

The Three Palaces of Karambitan

Karambitan, in the western regency of Tabanan, is the traditional home of powerbrokers of the Tabanan dynasty and an area full of surprises. It was once the home of kingmakers and a source of wives for kings all over Bali. Along with this power came wealth, and the three palaces of Karambitan reflect this in their maintenance of traditional architectural forms and garden styles.

Here you will find, in Puri Anyar and Puri Gede, some of the purest examples of traditional palace layout, original 1920s and '30s architecture, paintings for ceremonial pavilions, and a stupendous main shrine area, where the daring step of making ancestral images was first initiated by the late I Gusti Ktut Sangka and his father, I Gusti Gede Oka.

Modern Gardens in Bali

Very little of what might be called traditional Balinese gardening remains today. Government policies have been encouraging the Balinese to diversify their diets and grow a wider variety of plants in their yards, so their compounds are now often filled with tomatoes and herbs as well as fruit trees. Hot on the heels of this new health programme came a *tamanisasi* or "gardenisation" programme encouraging villagers to plant their own flower beds. The main æsthetic principle behind *tamanisasi* was order, so often messy trees which shed their leaves have been replaced by flower beds planted in neatly–ordered rows arranged by height.

Above: *Ruins at one of the most spectacular pleasure palaces, constructed by the beach near Ujung by the last ruler of the Karangasem dynasty. It was destroyed by earthquakes in the early 1980s.*

Contemporary Balinese Gardens

Picture, if you will, one of those great, eternally green glasshouses so popular in Victorian England, but magically enlarged to such an extent that it is capable of holding an entire island, volcanoes and all, with a plentiful supply of fertile soil and water from both sky and ever-flowing springs. Achieve such a feat of the imagination and then you will have a general idea of the dazzling range of possibilities that await any would-be gardener who sets out to exercise his talents on Bali.

The extraordinary ease and speed with which almost everything grows in such a setting means that gardens have always played a prominent role in Balinese life, whether arranged to enhance the splendours of its palaces and temples or merely haphazard collections of bananas, coconut palms, spices and other practical plants around the homes of ordinary people. The Dutch added different landscape concepts during their half-century of colonial rule over the island, while still others came in the early years of tourism. The greatest number of gardens, certainly the most impressive in terms of design and plant material, have been established only within the past few decades and reflect a whole new era in horticultural development.

Those responsible for these contemporary gardens represent an assortment of nationalities. Balinese have drawn on their intimate knowledge of local conditions to create many, either for their own use or for outsiders less skilled. Residents of neighbouring Java or from nearby countries with similar climates have also found fresh sources of inspiration on the island. Others have come from much more distant places and been stirred by a perhaps unexpected urge to express themselves through the medium of plants.

Despite its relatively small size, Bali's striking differences in climate and topography present the gardener with a wide range of possibilities. The hilly countryside near Ubud, for instance, with its steep ravines and meandering streams, offers an opportunity for dramatic multi-level plantings and views of breathtaking beauty. At still higher elevations on the rich slopes of the island's looming volcanoes, where temperatures drop much lower than in the lowlands, it is possible to have a European garden of roses, azaleas and fresh strawberries, though without having to contend with the long months of winter bleakness. Along some parts of the shore, at such popular beach resorts as Sanur and Kuta, monsoon rains bring a steamy atmosphere of fecundity that

Opposite: *The pool and poolside* balé *at the house of Carlo Pessina in Sanur Different varieties of pandanus grow abundantly on the right, while coconut palms throw shade on the left.*

Above: *A* balé *in the grounds of the house of Philip Lakeman and Graham Oldroyd in Ubud. A variegated Agave provides drama in the foreground, while ever-blooming* Russelia equisetiformis *gives colour behind.*

encourages mini-jungles to grow almost overnight; other coastal areas like Nusa Dua, on the other hand, are notably dry and demand a different sort of gardening approach.

Individual tastes in design also vary. Some seek to emulate the rather formal patterns of a traditional Balinese arrangement, making use of water, courtyards, statuary and a limited number of strategically placed plants. Others prefer a more "natural" effect, in which the garden merges with the surrounding country-side so that it is difficult to discern where one stops and the other begins; this is particularly popular in the hill country, where features like Bali's celebrated rice terraces are sufficiently spectac-ular not to require much embellishment.

Perhaps the majority of those who come from less hospitable climates, however, are so stimulated by their discovery of so much sheer botanical exuberance, and by what the 19th-century traveller Isabella Bird called "all the promise of perpetual spring and the fulfillment of endless summer" that they are tempted to produce theatrical settings of maximum tropic luxuriance with huge, decorative leaves, brilliant flowers and tangled creepers crowding close and often into the buildings they adorn.

Thanks not only to such hospitable growing conditions but also to the comparative ease with which plants can now be moved over great distances, Balinese gardens today display much more variety than in the past. New ornamentals are constantly being introduced by individual collectors, more often than not through landscapes like those shown on the following pages; for a rainy season or two they take pride of place, admired as rare specimens in a private garden or as part of the landscape created for a resort hotel, and then assuming they flourish—as they nearly always do—they become part of the plant material available to all.

Thus the possibilities multiply and the already magical gardens of Bali acquire an added richness to inspire future generations who fall under their spell.

Right: *A meandering portion of the Water Garden at the Bali Hyatt designed by Made Wijaya, a classic example of his artful natural style.*
Overleaf: *The lily pond at the Grand Hyatt garden in Nusa Dua echoes the design of royal Balinese pleasure gardens. The lily is a sacred plant where deities and heavenly nymphs are thought to rest.*

Gardens in Sanur

Sanur, with its long expanse of tempting white sand along a tranquil, reef-sheltered lagoon, has been a favoured retreat among both tourists and long-staying Bali lovers for over fifty years and is generally regarded as the island's first beach resort. On or near the coast, half-hidden in groves of venerable trees and rustling coconut palms, can be found some of the most luxurious hotels, guest houses and private villas. These have some of Bali's loveliest gardens, plantings that have helped define the possibilities of contemporary landscape design in a tropical setting.

Sanur History

There is an older past as well, however, less evident to the casual visitor strolling past the souvenir shops on Jalan Danau Tamblingan, the main street, or sipping an afternoon drink on a breezy terrace overlooking the sea. Ancient, ornately decorated temples are scattered all along the shore, sometimes within the compounds of modern hotels surrounded by walls made of coral and noted for the exuberance of their annual festival. Sanur itself, once part of the kingdom of Badung, is still one of Bali's last remaining villages controlled by members of the Brahman priestly caste. The oldest inscribed pillar in Bali, dated A.D. 913, is kept in a temple at the village of Belanjong in southern Sanur; it records the story of a Javanese king who came to the island and founded a Buddhist monastery, evidence of a highly developed culture nearly a thousand years ago.

In 1904, a Chinese trading ship was wrecked off Sanur's reef. The refusal of the king of Badung to accept responsibility for the lost cargo provided the Dutch with a pretext for military action

Opposite: *Stone statuary, such as this whimsical frog which is the work of renowned Ubud sculptor Wayan Cemul, is an integral part of many Balinese gardens today. The unusual thatched guest bungalows at Taman Mertasari in Sanur echo the design of the Balinese rice barn or* lumbung *which was traditionally used to store the annual harvest and seed for next year's planting.*

Top right: *A painting of the luxurious Batujimbar residential complex at Sanur, by Australian artist Donald Friend, who lived here in the 1960s and '70s (courtesy of the Neka Museum, Ubud).*

Bottom right: *Sunrise on the beach at Sanur highlights the outrigger canoes ideal for water-borne explorations of the reef.*

two years later. Landing on the beach, they marched for four days of hard fighting to nearby Denpasar and the royal palace enclosure. Here they were greeted by a strange, silent procession led by the king and his family, all dressed in white but richly ornamented and armed with lances and ceremonial *kris*. "One hundred paces from the startled Dutch," according to one account, "the *radja* halted his bearers, stepped from his palanquin, gave the signal and the ghastly ceremony began. A priest plunged his dagger into the *radja's* breast, and others of the company began turning their daggers upon themselves or upon one another." Still others rushed in a blind frenzy at the invaders, who proceeded to open fire with cannons and guns that killed over a thousand men, women and children, the most notorious of the *puputans* or fights to the death, that finally brought Bali under colonial control.

Dawn of the Tourist Age

The life style for which Sanur is famous today began soon after the start of tourism. The earliest visitors came by KPM, the Dutch steamship line, disembarking at Buleleng in the north and then being driven south to Denpasar where the Bali Hotel was opened in 1925. Most stayed only for a standard five-day visit, but a few of the more adventurous and romantic lingered much longer, enchanted by the Bali they gradually discovered, and these were largely responsible for the books, photographs, and paintings that made its charms legendary throughout the world.

The popular writer Vicki Baum (author of *Grand Hotel*) produced a novel, *A Tale from Bali*, about the tragic 1906 *puputan*. So did the

Left: *A huge* Waringin *or* Banyan *tree, its aerial roots almost orange in colour, dominates a corner of the garden of La Taverna.*

Right Top: *The house and garden of Belgian painter Adrien Le Mayeur de Merprès, located on the beach just to the north of the Grand Bali Beach hotel, is now a museum; the cup-shaped leaf on the left (Polysias scutellaria), behind the Crotons, is used as a herb in some parts of Indonesia.*

Right: *A romantic corner of the garden at Taman Sari, one of the earliest resorts at Sanur Beach, whose overgrown pathways and charming, thatched-roof bungalows each set in its own private garden, helped give birth to a new style of Balinese architecture and decor. This style emphasises structures that are more in harmony with the natural landscape and traditional culture.*

Above: *The use of blocks of coral as a building material in Sanur, such as for this wall at Batujimbar, has now been discontinued to protect the reefs.*
Right: *A fine antique door used as a garden gate is flanked by weathered volcanic-stone statues, Red Hibiscus and Bougainvillea.*

Mexican-born painter Miguel Covarrubias, whose illustrated travel book about the island is still widely read. Other visitors included the Woolworth heiress Barbara Hutton, the anthropologist Margaret Mead, as well as celebrities like Charlie Chaplin and Noel Coward.

Some of these notable visitors found the paradise they sought in the hills around Ubud, where the German artist Walter Spies made himself the influential centre of a group devoted to the study of Balinese art and culture. Others, though, went no further from Denpasar than the sun-dappled sands of neighbouring Sanur. Two German brothers, Hans and Rolf Neuhaus, opened an aquarium and art shop there in 1935 and became the leading dealers in Balinese paintings and wood-carvings, while the American Jack Mershon and his choreographer wife Katharane (with whom Spies devised the now-famous *kecak* or "monkey" dance) built one of the first bungalows on the beach. A Belgian aristocrat, Adrien Le Mayeur de Merprès, became a resident painter and married a beautiful young dancer who became his chief model.

Sanur's popularity with international travellers returned after World War II and the struggle for Indonesian independence. Charming bungalow-style hotels appeared, often featuring Balinese architecture and decor and set in gardens of uncommon beauty. The artistic tradition was continued by two Australian painters, Donald Friend and Ian Fairweather, who built homes on the sea; Friend's bungalow boasted a superb collection of art, a huge garden of exotic plants and a resident *gamelan* orchestra to entertain guests. Sanur's reputation as a centre of music and dance also survived; there are still theatrical performances of one kind or another almost every night and frequent temple festivals.

The first modern hotel was the multi-storied Bali Beach. This was built in the early 1960s during the Sukarno era with Japanese reparations money; it aimed at well-heeled tourists who (so it was thought) demanded up-to-date Western amenities. It turned out, however, that many preferred plainer bungalow-type structures more in harmony with the natural landscape and traditional culture. These remain the norm for Sanur, as exemplified by the Tanjung Sari, which is a complex of sumptuous bungalows built to offer both comfort and a memorably Balinese atmosphere. Eventually a government regulation was passed forbidding any

construction taller than the height of a mature coconut palm, thus assuring the preservation of Sanur's special village character.

Sanur Gardens Today

The area's contemporary gardens vary widely in size and mood. Of those associated with hotels, the 36-acre Bali Hyatt garden is not only the largest by far but also the most beautiful and influential; a number of new ornamental plants were introduced to the island here and the impressive design concepts have inspired a host of others. The winding pathways, moss-covered coral walls and jungle-like atmosphere of the Tanjung Sari have also served as models for similar concepts where each guest room is a separate, private structure with its own decorative plantings.

When he died in the late 1950s, after 26 years in Bali, Adrien Le Mayeur left his house to the Indonesian government. Located near the Bali Beach Hotel, the house and the statue-filled garden from which he drew inspiration are now preserved as a museum.

Left: *A kulkul or alarm tower constructed of coral blocks and surrounded by shrubs and coconut palms stands at the end of the pool in the holiday home of Michelle Han and Tony Turner of Hong Kong, located in the exclusive Batujimbar complex at Sanur.*

Above: *At night, the coconut palms surrounding the house become feathery silhouettes, whereas the pool itself takes on an eery glow due to the blocks of grey-green slate used as the pool lining.*

Top: *The house of hotelier and restaurateur Rodolfo Giusti, who has created several gardens in Bali, and whose house on the beach in Sanur seems almost engulfed by the luxuriant garden.*

Above: *Pavilions, walkways and lotus ponds of the celebrated Lotus Restaurant in Sanur, designed by Rodolfo Giusti.*

Left and Opposite: *The garden in front of Giusti's house in Sanur, created with Made Wijaya, reflects his passion for the lotus and fondness for large jars as a garden decoration.*

Batujimbar, where Donald Friend once lived in such splendour, has become one of Bali's most exclusive private estates: a dozen or so elegant villas where members of the jet set come to relax, away from worldly pressures. Gardens play a major part in Batujimbar's charm, with well-tended lawns linking some houses while others achieve added privacy behind the vine-draped coral walls characteristic of Sanur. Among the plants that give the estate its luxuriant atmosphere are bright-coloured Cordylines and Codiaeums, Red Ginger, Plumeria, ornamental bananas, Bird's Nest Ferns and a wide range of creepers, as well as numerous shady trees and coconut palms.

Away from the beach, mostly hidden by walls along narrow, palm-fringed lanes, can be glimpsed other imaginative gardens of relatively recent origin. One example is called Taman Mertasari, "Garden of Holy Water Essence" and consists of several Balinese-style houses. Central features of the compound are a traditional thatched-roof rice barn and a large lotus pond out of which several of the property's original coconut palms grow on islands.

Another celebrated Sanur garden is the Villa Bebek, the atelier-home of Made Wijaya, or Michael White as he was known in his native Australia. Wijaya has lived in Bali since 1973 and created his first garden around an earlier house, also in Sanur; this attracted so much admiration that he later became a professional full-time designer who has played a significant role in the development of tropical landscapes not only on the island but also in other parts of Indonesia as well as Singapore, Thailand, and the Caribbean (where he planted the home of pop star David Bowie). His Balinese contributions include a major restoration of the Bali Hyatt garden in the early 1980s, the recent Four Seasons Hotel at Jimbaran on the Bukit Peninsula, and numerous private gardens for both permanent and part-time residents.

Left Above: *This open doorway at Taman Mertasari is almost lost amidst greenery, including palms and Scindapsus climbing the tree to the right.*
Left: *A floating pavilion crowded by aquatic plants and bordered by statues provides a tranquil area for relaxation.*
Right: *The swimming pool at Taman Mertasari, with an antique door separating it from another house within the overall compound. The yellow trumpet-like flowers to the left are Allamanda.*

The Villa Bebek is a characteristically Balinese arrangement of courtyards that offer both privacy and a sense of surprise, with lush planting that sets off cooling ponds. The labyrinthine complex is a veritable mini village of courtyards, ponds, gates and walls, along with ten buildings each accompanied by numerous terraces. Among the specimens used for its jungle–like effect are Alpinia, dwarf Bamboo, assorted ferns, Plumeria, coconut palms, and fragrant, night–blooming creepers, as well as a wide range of water plants.

In addition to being Wijaya's principal residence, the Villa Bebek compound also serves as an office and workshop for a team of designers and local artisans who are responsible for the distinctive architectural features and art works that adorn Wijaya's gardens. He freelay admits that his own gardens are a constant work in progress, with niches, courts and pools being planted and re–planted when a new light or a new planter arrives. Wijaya sees them as a testing ground for his team. Having said that, some elements are static. An azure lap pool–enticing, fresh, modern, Hockneyesque even–is the centre-

Left: *A pond in the garden of the Villa Bebek in Sanur, atelier-home of the landscape designer Made Wijaya; among the plants that contribute to the luxuriant effect are Alpinia purpurata, Iris, Bamboo and Maidenhair and Fishtail Ferns.*
Above: *Balinese girls place traditional offerings near the Villa Bebek pond.*

piece, and the villas gather around this. Attendant to this is a folly–like water tower with panels by sculptor Wayan Cemul and the breakfast nook set beneath a premier pergola shaded by cascading white *Thunbergia grandiflora*.

Wijaya's creative input on projects encompasses pathways, walls, pavilions, walls, and other components, as well as the less permanent "soft" landscape. Gateways, for example, which he calls the "tiaras of courtyard architecture", are a speciality; he says he has designed more than 50 for various compounds, in almost every material from coral to red brick. Garden ornaments and statues produced under his supervision include lighting fixtures, sculptures, fountains, bird–baths, and assorted other items, now being internationally marketed under a company called the Wijaya Classics Range.

Such landscapes, public and private, reflect the continuing appeal of Sanur's tropical abundance and suggest that it is likely to survive any developments the future might hold.

Above: Antique Balinese door at the house of Bruce Carpenter in Sanur; the mud wall and alang alang *covering is based on a simple, traditional design.*
Above right: The compound is divided into three sections; this antique gebyog *door separates the eastern and western parts of the garden.*
Right: Detail of an antique volcanic stone statue from Gianyar Regency, holding a holy water container with amrita, the elixer of the gods.
Opposite: A marble-topped colonial table is combined with iron and rattan chairs on the dining verandah. The floor has celadon and yellow tiles.

The Bali Hyatt Garden

The close integration of landscape and architecture, sometimes so intimately that the former predominates from a visual standpoint, is a concept well suited to the tropics. Certainly some of its most memorable realisations can be found in those places where a benign climate encourages outdoor living all year round and where rich supplies of ever-growing, highly decorative plant materials are readily at hand.

Traditional palaces, temples and homes in many cultures provide classic models of such life styles; Balinese temples and palaces, for example, were compositions that made maximum use of water, trees and plants harmoniously arranged around airy open pavilions. Others have been the product of individual, even eccentric vision. On a small island off the southern coast of Sri Lanka, in the 1920s, a Swiss aristocrat carried the concept to what was possibly its ultimate extreme by building an octagonal house that had no walls at all, even for the bathrooms, so that views of the surrounding sea and jungle garden were completely unimpeded. The result, according to the writer Paul Bowles, who later lived there, was "very rational and, like most things born of fanaticism, wildly impractical".

In more contemporary times, resort hotels have emerged as leaders in the exploration of innovative ways to merge nature with the work of man—not surprisingly, perhaps, given the prominence of a romantic atmosphere in their appeal to travellers. None have been willing to go quite as far as the aristocratic dreamer in Sri Lanka, but they have nevertheless been responsible for some memorable creations against tropical backgrounds ranging from the Caribbean to the Pacific. One of the most notable Asian examples, acknowledged as a landmark and pace setter for nearly thirty years, is the spectacular Bali Hyatt at Sanur.

An Evolving Garden

Construction of the Bali Hyatt began in the early 1970s on a 36-acre former coconut plantation facing the sea, one of the prime locations at the island's oldest beach resort. From the beginning, the designers determined that landscape would be a central

Left: *Red Ginger* (Alpinia purpurata) *dominates the foreground of the lush Matahari Garden at the Bali Hyatt.*

Top: *The kulkul tower at the entrance to the resort, surrounded by a lotus pond; a traditional decoration hangs from the bamboo pole on the right.*
Right: *Girls carrying offerings made from folded palm leaves and flowers. In the background are* Ravenala madagascariensis, *Traveller's Palms.*
Opposite: *A procession moves down the entrance drive of the resort on its way to a ceremony.* Vernonia elaeaguifolia, *the hanging creeper, is widely known in Southeast Asia as "Lee Kuan Yew" because of its popularity in Singapore.*

feature, occupying 75 per cent of the total area and utilising huge planter boxes, jungle–like courtyards and water gardens to further soften and in places almost obscure the deliberately simple lines of the modern, low–rise guest wings built around courts. One of the architects, Kerry Hill of Australia, explained the objective as "a dramatic celebration with the garden almost threatening the open spaces in the architecture".

This sense of drama is particularly strong in the hotel lobby, essentially a vast breezy pavilion with a soaring pitched roof made of coconut beams covered with thatched elephant grass. The spacious feeling is enhanced by the gleaming wood floors, the subdued traditional furnishings and most of all, two completely open sides that afford unobstructed views of the magnificent garden. Each of the guest rooms also has a balcony from which to survey the greenery to maximum advantage, while the Regency Club, a virtually self–contained group of 50 deluxe rooms, is built around a cool water garden.

Ketut Reilly, a Balinese graduate in landscape architecture from the prestigious Trisakti University in Jakarta, was in charge of the initial planting to achieve this effect. Many of the larger trees and palms installed by him can be seen growing on the site today. The present views, though, are not merely somewhat more established versions of those admired by the first guests present at the resort's opening back in 1973. Tropical gardens alter at a very different rate from their temperate counterparts, with growth being measured by single rainy seasons rather than

Top: The garden overlooking the small golf course at the Bali Hyatt
Above: A Flame Tree (Delonix regia) in bloom at the end of the dry season.
Opposite: White Plumeria and scarlet Flame Tree, two of Bali's most decorative trees; in the bed below are Codiaeum, Cordylines, Arundodonax and a ground cover of Rhoeo.

generations. The relatively small tree of today is likely to become a towering giant in the space of only a few years, shrubs mature within a single season and ground covers quickly escape their allotted spaces and require almost daily attention. Individual effects are thus constantly changing and only by continual cutting back and replanting could the original ones be preserved.

At the Bali Hyatt, such changes are accepted less as problems than as an inevitable part of the garden's evolution, a natural process that will continue in the future and result in still different but equally enticing vistas. Major landscape revisions were undertaken in the early 1980s under the supervision of the noted landscape designer Made Wijaya and his associate Ketut Marsa. These consisted of a dramatic series of new terraces off the lobby, the addition of special botanical and theme gardens near the golf course, and replanting of the guest wing courts. There were other, lesser alterations during renovation of the hotel in 1994. The original concept of architecture almost engulfed by natural greenery has remained what it was from the start, however, and will only be embellished by the nourishing monsoon rains of years to come.

Varied Vistas and Botanical Curiosities

The Bali Hyatt landscape today offers not only a comprehensive collection of ornamental plants gathered from many parts of the tropical world (some 500 different species according to the latest estimate), but also a beguiling variety of moods. There are sunny, open expanses and intimate, semi-private areas; pathways that wind through jungle-like luxuriance and others along the long seafront; bold splashes of colour and restful masses of green, all with shifting patterns of sunlight and shade and cooling glimpses of half a dozen pools and waterways.

A tour of the garden's botanical delights might begin at the stone *kulkul* tower, inspired by those used in Balinese temples for alarm drums, which stands at the entrance. As in temples, the tower seems to float in a surrounding pond planted with *Nelumbo nucifera*, the sacred pink lotus, "the fairest flower of the East" according to one writer and, by any reckoning, the most famous. For more than 5,000 years, the lotus has captured the imagination of a wide variety of cultures, especially Hindu and Buddhist, who have found compelling symbolism in both its beauty and its growing habits.

Below: *A Balinese lantern surrounded by a luxuriant mass of plants and shaded by coconut palms that are a dominant feature of the landscape.*
Opposite: *Terraces off one of the guest wings, where the foreground is dominated by red and green Alternanthera and white Arundodonax versicolor. In the background can be seen Red Ginger and the orange flowers of Caesalpinia pulcherrima.*

To Buddhists in particular, its appearance from the murky depths of a pool proclaims the power of the soul to rise out of the darkness of evil into the pure light of *nirvana*, while the wheel–like shape of its five flower petals represents the doctrine of endless cycles of existence. The simultaneous appearance of seed pod, blossom and bud is a convenient suggestion of past, present, and future. Even the non–wettable quality of the leaves–due to a network of microscopic hairs–is seen as significant, inspiring a chant that goes "May my soul resemble the gem–like dewdrop which lies on the lip of the lotus leaf before it falls into the peaceful obscurity of the lake".

Balinese Hindus, who call it *tanjung*, have a similarly reverent attitude toward the lotus, using it in offerings as well as depicting it in temple decorations and other forms of art. Here as elsewhere, the plant also plays a more practical role in daily life since every part, from the underground tubers to the seeds, can be eaten or used as medicine.

From the tower, a pathway leads off into the front garden where a small, meticulously maintained golf course serves a double purpose as a recreation facility for guests and also, from a design standpoint, as a lawn to accentuate the massed plantings on all sides. Many of the original trees can be seen in this area, having by now reached their full maturity after two decades of growth. Coconut palms, survivors of the more than 2,000 that originally grew on the site, predominate, as they do all over Sanur and other parts of Bali as well. Locally known as *nyuh*, the coconut is essential to Balinese life, providing building materials as well as food and drink. On plantations, growers make regular offerings to ensure a bountiful crop of nuts which, on a good palm, can mean up to 100 a year for as long as 50 years.

Numerous ornamental specimens were also added during the initial landscaping for their periodic displays of colour. The Flame Tree or Royal Poinciana (*Delonix regia*), for example, is transformed toward the end of the dry season into a dazzling canopy of scarlet, orchid–like blossoms, while the Indian Laburnum (*Cassia fistula*) produces long cascades of golden–yellow flowers. Other ornamentals include the fragrant Plumeria; the Erythrina or Coral Tree, of which several varieties are found in Bali and which is regarded as a life symbol because of the speed with which cuttings root and grow; the yellow Acacia, a member of the Mimosa

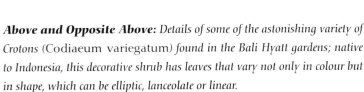

Above and Opposite Above: *Details of some of the astonishing variety of* Crotons (Codiaeum variegatum) *found in the Bali Hyatt gardens; native to Indonesia, this decorative shrub has leaves that vary not only in colour but in shape, which can be elliptic, lanceolate or linear.*

Opposite Below: *The "Yellow Garden" is made up of a variety of plants, including Crotons and* Pseuderanthemum reticulatum.

family and a relatively recent introduction to the island; and the slender stalks of the Betel Nut Palm (*Areca catechu*), whose bright orange fruit is highly prized by the remaining *betel*–chewers throughout Southeast Asia.

Ficus trees are also seen here as in most parts of the garden– not the small, lovingly–tended house plants common to so many Western living rooms but robust giants that form an impressive spread of dense leaves. One species, *F. benjamina*, known to Bali- nese as the *Waringin*, is regarded as sacred and can be found in or near most of the island's temples and palaces, where its multiple trunks and aerial roots create mysterious, spirit–haunted caves as it increases in age. Another, *F. elastica*, which grows wild from India to Java, has much larger, glossy leaves; called the India Rubber Tree by indoor gardeners, it was indeed the principal source of rubber in Asia before the introduction of *Hevea brasilien- sis* at the end of the last century.

Here and there the large, pale–yellow leaves of Pisonia, the Lettuce Tree, stand out in contrast against the surrounding green, Fish–tail Palms (*Caryota mitis*) raise tufts of intricately–shaped fronds and Breadfruit trees (*Artocarpus altilis*) offer welcome shade beneath their capacious branches and shiny foliage. (While paus- ing briefly to escape the sun under one of the Breadfruits, a visi- tor might recall that early European voyagers were so impressed by this native of Polynesia from which "bread itself is gathered as fruit" that they decided to introduce it as a food crop for planta- tion labourers in the West Indies. In 1789, the *H.M.S. Bounty* was

Top: Cordyline terminalis, *popularly called the Ti plant, has a wide range of leaf colours and patterns.*

Above: Agave angustifolia, *a variegated variety with sharp decorative spines, which produces a tall flower just before dying.*

Opposite: *A courtyard planting. The ground cover for the central bed is Pedilanthus, while Scindapsus is employed on the left; other plants include red Cordylines, Agaves, fan palms, Bamboo and Plumeria.*

attempting to transport Breadfruit seedlings from Tahiti to Kew Gardens when the celebrated mutiny took place.)

As strikingly tropical as the coconut palm in any larger garden like the Bali Hyatt's is *Ravenala madagascariensis*, popularly known as the Traveller's Palm. This is actually not a palm at all but a member of the banana family. Rising from a tall trunk, it spreads a spectacular fan of enormous, paddle–shaped leaves that are used as thatch in some parts of the tropics. The popular name comes from the fact that pure water accumulates at the base of the leaves and can be drawn on by thirsty strangers in times of drought.

An oddity worth looking out for is *Kigelia pinnata*, the Sausage Tree, a native of tropical West Africa which was brought to the Bali Hyatt from the great botanical garden at Bogor in Java. The fruits of this horticultural curiosity do indeed resemble huge sausages, sometimes up to half a metre long, dangling from the tree on long stems. The large velvety flowers, yellow outside and dark red within, also hang like chandeliers and have an unpleasant smell that attracts the insects necessary for cross–pollination.

Special Plantings

A section of the front garden consists of plantings linked by pathways and devoted to a special theme or a particular ornamental group. Some of the plants here were first introduced to the island at the Bali Hyatt, having been brought from elsewhere in Indonesia or other tropical places like Singapore and Hawaii.

A gateway covered with white *Thunbergia grandiflora*, for instance, leads to a rather formal arrangement around an octagonal lily pond graced by a vaguely European-looking statue. "After Vita" proclaims a sign above the entrance–enigmatically, perhaps, to some visitors, though certainly not to anyone familiar with Sissinghurst, the famous creation of the horticulturist Victoria Sackville–West and her husband, Harold Nicholson, in the English countryside. Among the most celebrated features of Sissinghurst is its White Garden and here, on a much smaller scale, is Made Wijaya's tropical equivalent, planted with such carefully-selected specimens as white–blooming Bougainvillea, Plumeria, Hibiscus, Gardenia, water lilies and assorted other shrubs and ground covers that have pale or variegated foliage.

Elsewhere in the same area there are collections of such foliage shrubs as Cordyline and Codiaeum in a spectrum of bright

colours, Heliconias and Gingers which flower most profusely in the wet season, rare palms, cacti, and Bromeliads. There is also a mossy, secluded terrace where a lush display of Bird's Nest Ferns and similar plants festoons the trunks of trees. These are located around an aviary containing exotic birds.

A series of broad terraces extending down over several levels from the front of the main building to the golf course has been transformed through imaginative planting into huge, swirling patterns of colour that resemble the creations of an abstract painter. The best vantage point from which to view the dramatic effect of this area is from the Bali Hyatt lobby or from the ramp leading to the guest wings.

Among the low plants employed for carpet-like effects and contrasts are Alternanthera, with both red and green-and-white leaves; metallic purple Hemigraphis; bright-green Wedelia; Pedilanthus, a green or variegated succulent sometimes called Japanese Poinsettia; *Rhoeo discolor*, on which the spiky leaves are dark green on top and purple below; Sansevieria, popularly known as Mother-in-Law's Tongue; Ophiopogon, which resembles a variegated grass when planted close together; a small variety of *Duranta repens* with bright yellow leaves and Scindapsus (now called Epipremnum by some horticulturists), variously known as the Money Plant, Golden Pothos and Devil's Ivy, which has glossy leaves of different colours and patterns and not only serves as a dense ground cover but also clambers up trees.

A bright splash is supplied by *Caesalpinia pulcherrima*, which is sometimes called the Dwarf Poinciana. This is a medium-sized shrub with an almost continual display of red-orange or yellow flowers that in form closely resemble those of *Delonix regia*; the Balinese name, *merak*, means "peacock", an appellation by which the plant is called in other places as well.

Larger plants, too, add dramatic colour to the terraces. One of the most spectacular is *Alpinia purpurata*, the Red Ginger. This plant, native to Melanesia and the Moluccas, is now found as an ornamental all over the tropics. It belongs to the Zingiberaceae family, which consists of some 50 genera and 1,000 species,

Left: Guest-wing garden with Heliconia on the left and Syngonium used as a ground cover; in the right foreground is a Philodendron bipinnatifidum.

Above: *A corner of the Matahari Garden where shrubs and creepers spill over the banks of a pond.*

Opposite: *The surface of this pond in the Matahari garden is almost completely covered by day-blooming water lilies.*

including the common edible ginger. On *A. purpurata*, the rich crimson "flowers" (actually stiff bracts) rise from the end of the leaf stalk and sometimes reach a foot in height; other varieties, which are not yet common in Bali, have pink or pure-white bracts. In Samoa, they are woven into *leis* for important ceremonies and denote rank, while elsewhere in the South Pacific they are transformed into an ornamental dress resembling chain mail. The Bali Hyatt was one of the first Balinese gardens to grow the handsome plant successfully on a large scale and still has some of the best plantings.

Botanically related to the Alpinia is the Heliconia, with equally impressive inflorescences that are generally red, yellow, orange, or combinations of all three. Indigenous to the American tropics, Heliconias prefer well-drained humid surroundings and so thrive in Bali, though to date relatively few of the more than 250 species have been introduced to the island. Several can be seen at the Bali Hyatt, including those with both erect and hanging inflorescences.

The apparent flowers of *Mussaenda philippica*, the Virgin Tree, which came originally from the Philippines, are actually bracts, in this case pink or white (occasionally red) with a velvety texture; Balinese call it *nusa indah*, "beautiful island", in a fitting tribute to the mass of delicate colour it brings to a garden.

A number of the terrace shrubs have been selected for their coloured foliage. Prominent among these is *Codiaeum variegatum* (Crotons), native to Indonesia; it has leaves in a wide range of hues and shapes. Another plant native to Malaysia, Indonesia, and the South Pacific is *Cordyline terminalis*. On the latter, the colour of the leaves occur from bright red to patterns of green and white. Hawaiians, who call it the *Ti* plant, believe that the red variety invites misfortune if grown near a home; Malays, on the other hand, believe that it dispels evil spirits and so should be planted as closely as possible, as it is in many Balinese gardens. (Old-fashioned Chinese believe to be a sign of good luck when the plant flowers, a phenomenon that—alas—occurs only rarely.) *Acalypha wilkesiana* provides an equally large variety of leaf colours and, unlike Cordylines, it does best in full sunlight and so is planted in the lower, more open areas at the Bali Hyatt. A bamboo-like reed called *Arundodonax versicolor*, with almost pure white leaves, also makes a dramatic statement in sunny areas,

while *Polyscias fruticosa* (Panax) is used to provide a light green background and a wide range of leaf forms.

Hymenocallis and Crinum are used for mass effects here as elsewhere in the garden. Though both are popularly called Spider Lilies, they are in fact different plants, the strap-shaped leaves emerging straight from underground tubers on the first and, on the second, forming a large crown at the top of a thick stalk. The flowers of both are delightfully scented after dark.

The Guest-wing Courtyards

Each of the Bali Hyatt's three guest-wing courtyards has been named after a plant, which are depicted on the carved room keys and left on pillows as offerings when beds are turned down for the night. All three were actually introduced to Bali from else-where, but so long ago that they are now found growing almost wild and have become an integral part of local life.

No Balinese garden, for example, would be complete without at least one and usually several kinds of Hibiscus, whose brightly coloured flowers are used in nearly all ceremonies as well as for personal adornment. *H. rosa-sinensis*, the most common species, may have originated in China as the scientific name suggests, though wild specimens have much smaller flowers than the hybrids usually seen throughout the tropics today. The Balinese call it *pucuk*, the "shoe flower," an odd name which some say is derived from an old Portuguese custom of blackening their shoes with a juice made from the petals. Another species, *H. schizopetalus*, native to East Africa, has flowers with lacy petals and a long pistil; in Bali, this species is associated with magic, particularly of the darker sort. At the Bali Hyatt some of the red Hibiscus have been trained to grow to a considerable height up the guest-wing walls, mingling with the other true creepers such as *Thunbergia grandiflora*, which has clusters of pale blue flowers.

Frangipani Court was inspired by the Plumeria, a New World native probably brought to Asia by early European explorers. Named after the French botanist Charles Plumier–the earliest spelling of the genus was in fact Plumieria–it allegedly acquired

Left: *Colourful lawn with red Hibiscus,* Delonix regia, *Plumeria and blue* Plumbago auriculata *in the foreground.*

its common name because its fragrance reminded Europeans of a perfume invented by the Italian Frangipani family four centuries before the tree was discovered. Another theory, however, asserts that the thick white latex that flows when a branch is cut reminded French settlers in the Caribbean of *frangipanier*, French for coagulated milk. Several varieties are found growing almost everywhere in Bali, where the general name is *jepun*, and its pure flowers–especially white, the most strongly scented–are used for a wide assortment of ceremonial and decorative purposes.

The third court is Bougainvillea, named after the brilliant creeper that spills over many of the balconies of the Bali Hyatt. Indigenous to Brazil, Bougainvillea is particularly well–suited to seaside gardens since its coloured bracts appear most profusely in dry, sunny locations. The natural colour is purple, but count-less variants are available, from pure white to bright crimson and several that have two colours on the same plant; there is also a variety with double bracts. The *B. glabra* variety blooms year-round in Southeast Asia, while *B. spectabilis*, flowers best only in the dry season. Balinese call Bougainvillea *kertas*, "paper", which refers to the texture of the bracts.

Left: *This temple, one of many old temples located along Sanur beach, now lies within the grounds of the Bali Hyatt; priests still come here to pray.*
Above: *Offerings are placed daily in shrines and at important points through-out every structure in Bali to appease the unseen spirits.*

Besides the plants after which they are named, the courtyards are planted with a dense mixture so as to present an assortment of textures and colours when seen either from above or along the pathways that lead through them. Typical specimens include Red Gingers, Heliconias, Cordylines, ferns, the self–heading *Philodendron bipinnatifidum*, Crinum, variegated Agaves, taller trees and palms and assorted ground covers to create carpets.

Water Features

Water plays a significant role in nearly all Balinese gardens and the Bali Hyatt is no exception. Beginning with the lotus pond at the base of the *kulkul* tower at the entrance, other such features are scattered throughout the landscape, some of them prominent and others that come as serendipitous discoveries half hidden by dense masses of surrounding shrubbery and ground covers.

The Regency Club is almost surrounded by water in an evocation of classic palace gardens, the banks softened by planting that spills down to the water. From the lobby and ground–floor restaurants of the main building, there are views of cool ponds filled with blooming water lilies, while a stream wandering

Left and Below: *The walkway along Sanur Beach at the Bali Hyatt. An avenue of wind resisting* Calophyllum inophyllum, *running parallel to the beachfront, provides a convenient windbreak which protects the delicate flowering shrubs in the lawns behind. Several varieties of Pandanus and Agave reinforce the barrier against salty breezes.*

through the jungle garden can be glimpsed from bridges. Notable among the plants commonly seen near these informal water features is *Acrostichum aureum*, commonly known as the Giant Mangrove Fern, whose microscopic spores spread freely and take root in any available moist crevice, where their reddish new leaves drooping green fronds quickly reach an often impressive size, adding to the appearance of tropical abundance.

The resort's two swimming pools, each with its own distinctive atmosphere, should be included among the water features. The smaller one, fed by decorative terracotta fountains, surrounds a thatched-roof Balinese pavilion that appears to be floating on the blue water. The other, with green tiles, has an atmospheric grotto at the base of a luxuriantly planted hill, elaborate carvings of fierce-faced guardians and, between towering coconut palms, views of the sea as well as of the resort's sweeping lawns.

An Orderly Jungle

As seen from the terrace projecting out from the hotel lobby, the garden that crowds around the eastern side of the buildings has the appearance of a small jungle, more orderly than a real rainforest, perhaps, but still an impressive display of tropical abundance. The large yellow and green leaves of Scindapsus ascend the trunks of coconut palms, Red Ginger bracts flash in the dappled sunlight, ferns droop from crevices, scores of other shrubs and ground covers intermingle to form a nearly solid mass, broken here and there by a pool of blooming water lilies.

Left: The Regency Club, surrounded by a water garden like the classical floating pavilions of traditional Balinese Palaces.
Above: The Telaga Naga or Dragon Lake restaurant at dusk.

By day the varied shades of green and flowers create a living panorama to be enjoyed while relaxing on the terrace, by night a somewhat mysterious tangle illuminated by the soft light of strategically placed Balinese-style lanterns.

A more intimate aspect is seen from the ground level, where walkways bordered by high coral walls lead in a shadowy, labyrinth-like network out into the more open sea-front garden. Here the mini-jungle looms from overhead, spilling over the walls and mingling with various creepers. Prominent among the latter is a vigorous woody climber with small, willow-like leaves called *Vernonia elaeaguifolia* by botanists and in some parts of Southeast Asia widely known as "Lee Kuan Yew", since the former Prime Minister of Singapore allegedly encouraged its planting on a large scale in the island republic to hide unsightly walls. The story may be apocryphal, but it is certainly popular in Singapore. At the Bali Hyatt it is used extensively to soften walls and to trail in a decorative fashion from planter boxes.

Left: *At dawn, the swimming pool at the Bali Hyatt is magical, with coconut palms outlined against the sky; the "hair" of the stone demon guarding the pool grotto is a creeper,* Vernonia elaeaguifolia, *with a stand of Pandanus on the top.*
Above: *Sanur Beach seen from the pool at sunrise, with the sacred Mount Agung visible in the distance.*

The Seaside Garden

For all its scenic charms, an exposed seafront presents countless challenges to designers of tropical gardens and the Bali Hyatt was no exception. Twenty–odd years ago when construction started on the resort, the only real screen against the strong, salty winds was provided by tall coconut palms already growing profusely on the site. A number of plants common to Pacific beaches were incorporated into the design because of their ability to withstand seaside conditions (as well as their decorative appearance). One of these, a species of pandanus popularly called the Screwpine because of the way its spiky leaves emerge in a spiral arrangement at the ends of branches, grows here to a considerable height, putting out dramatic aerial roots for support. Also useful are *Terminalia catappa*, the Sea Almond, which takes a very distinctive pagoda–shape and has large leaves that turn autumnal colours in the dry season, *Crinum asiaticum*, native to Southeast Asia, and Scaevola, Sea Lettuce, a hardy shrub with pale green leaves that grows right down to the edge of the sea. *Calophyllum inophyllum* has formed a tall, shady avenue along the beach.

The most difficult part of the seafront garden was the area that now contains the outdoor restaurant. The sandy soil was thinner here than elsewhere and even normally tough wild trees took longer to become established. Now, however, they have attained an impressive size and provide shade as well as adequate protection for a garden of more delicate ornamentals nearby.

A Landmark Garden

Every morning more than 50 skilled gardeners begin the regular chores of raking, trimming, watering, replanting, and general maintenance that keep the Bali Hyatt garden in such admirable condition. An added dimension to the gardeners' labour is a sense of pride and awareness of being involved in something more than an ordinary landscape. For this is one of Bali's landmark gardens, a world–famous creation constantly evolving but always setting standards of beauty and imagination by which others are judged.

Top: *Typical outrigger canoes off Sanur, for touring over the coral reef.*
Above: *One of the two swimming pools at the Bali Hyatt resort.*
Opposite: *The seaside swimming pool, with its carved wall of volcanic stone.*

In Search of Ricefield Views

During the late 1960s long-term foreign residents began to drift westwards towards Kuta. Today, Kuta is Bali's most populous and frenetic tourist centre, but during the late 1960s and early '70s, it still had the feeling of a village; rows of coconut plantations separated it from the village of Legian to the north. Growth in the tourist market resulted in a spate of new construction; when the boom kept on going, it became difficult to tell where Kuta ended and Legian began. With the disappearance of the peace, privacy and affordable space for which Kuta had become famous, many decided to build their gardens further north, in Seminyak.

The northward and westward move continues, with land now being bought around Kerobokan and Canggu. At the time, these gardens frequently enjoyed tranquil vistas over the rice fields, vistas which inevitably disappeared as property values rose. These early Kuta gardens are all the more special because of their increasing rarity, while the newer gardens to the north allow owners to realise their dream of creating their own corner of paradise in Bali.

The search for tranquility has now extended as far as Tanah Lot and beyond. Here there are more of the coveted views of working rice fields, natural vegetation, and simple villages that first attracted outsiders to Bali. Creative gardeners in these newer areas are showing an appreciation for the native scenery and a tendency to incorporate it into their landscapes. At Le Meridien Resort, for example, overlooking Tanah Lot, paddy fields are an integral part of the golf course, and more and more private gardens are doing the same. Man-made features are being subordinated to the traditional scenery, or, where that is not possible, made as harmonious as is possible through the use of native materials and designs.

The paddy-shaped swimming pool is now common, as is a loose, open style of garden design that utilizes indigenous plants, many quite beautiful and exotic on their own. In these gardens the classic Balinese views are everything, a constant reminder of the unspoiled charm that so entranced the first Western visitors.

Left: *View of the pool at a house in Canggu. The shape of the pool mirrors the shape of the ricefield divisions in the background. The paving stones are* batu pilah, *a hard grey Balinese stone.*

Opposite: *The compound of Gianni Francione in the Kerobokan area. A stone walkway to one of the houses features palms and a colorful stand of yellow bamboo.*

Above: *Same compound, with stepping stones of grey* batu pilah *forming a geometric effect. The gardens were planted by Francione with the help of Braggy Latra, a local designer with a company called Lantana Indah.*

By the early '90s dream home makers were turning their attention to the picturesque rice field territory around Canggu well north of Seminyak and Legian. Here sumptious retreats arose, integrated with their rural settings–challenging their architects to learn a bit more about landscape. One such example is the home of Gianni Francione featured on pages 104–106. Another complex (pages 108–111) is the Puri Canggu Mertha built by the directors of Indonesia's biggest real estate firm. Pt Wijaya's offices (with Made Wijaya as principal designer) were appointed as architects, landscape and interior designers. Over a five–year period Wijaya designed a series of some eight–walled compounds set on a river meander that were contemporary in style with fresh clean interiors with modernist tromp l'oeil murals by artist Stephen Little. The villas opened out onto palatial gardens inspired by the water gardens of the early 20th–century kings of East Bali and Lombok. There are a series of garden surprises, encountered through a series of elaborate Balinese gates, and two pool courts; in many cases the landscape design creeps into the interiors, creating a harmonious whole to the entire complex.

Left: *A Plumeria tree droops decoratively over the swimming pool of Francione's garden. The garden ends right at the edge of a rice field and seems to incorporate it as part of the landscape design. A traditional-style balé echoes those seen and used in the adjacent fields.*

Above: *The Francione house, as seen from across the swimming pool.*

Left: *The gardens of the Canggu Puri Mertha, a hotel designed by Made Wijaya in Canggu. Stepping stones lead through the garden past a tiled pool, with a thatched pavilion in the background; the ceramic pots on the balustrade were made by artisans working for Made Wijaya as part of a series called Wijaya Classics.*

Above Top: *Russellia equisetiformis, popularly called the Coral Plant, is almost continuously in bloom. Here it tumbles down the side of a soapstone and limestone stairway leading to the swimming pool.*

Above: *View of the pool and pavilion; in the foreground can be seen the bright-red seed pods of Bixa orellana, from which a substance used as a food dye is extracted.*

Opposite: *In the same compound, an elaborate gate designed by Made Wijaya. On the right is a fragrant white Plumeria and below a clump of Rhapis elegans, a palm often used near the entrance to Balinese compounds.* **Above:** *Courtyard garden of the same compound. Russellia equisetiformis grows on the far side of the pool, while the limestone bird-bath on the right was produced by the Wijaya Classics Range of garden ornaments.*

Four Seasons Resort Bali at Jimbaran Bay

A different sort of terrain prevails south of Kuta and Jimbaran beaches, two of Bali's best beaches with scenic views of volcanoes across the sea. Here, on the Bukit Peninsula, in contrast to most of the island, the soil is sandy, lime-based and arid, scarcely what one might call ideally suited to a lush tropical garden. Yet that is what Made Wijaya has achieved on this 35-acre site, utilizing such drought-resistant plants as Bougainvillea, Agave, Adenium, Pandanus, and Plumeria, as well as numerous native species already growing there.

Nearly three and a half years under construction, the 147-villa resort was designed by Australian architects Martin Grounds and Jack Kent; up to 4,300 workers were employed on site and another 10,000 prepared materials elsewhere. It is laid out like a series of seven villages, each with its own distinctive atmosphere, surrounding the central facilities' building. Village lanes run east-west throughout, following the natural contours of the site, while dramatic stairs flow down the steep hillside north-south from the sea up to the highest point.

Within this scheme, guests are offered both sweeping views of the sea and the intimacy of private village courts with pools and fountains. Bright flowering creepers spill down sunny slopes, while tropical trees and shrubs provide shade and often fragrant flowers. Assorted works of art, nearly 1,500 in all, contribute to the Balinese atmosphere–Dewi Saraswati, goddess of gardens and art, as well as a large black stone face with buffalo horns and other statues are carved out of porous volcanic stone by the best local artisans, Wayan Cemul, Made Cangker and Nyoman Pergug.

Made Wijaya designed the spectacular gardens with Ir Ngurah Artawa, Dewar Sedana, Drs Nyoman Miyoga and 200 or so of his "commandoes"; they display his love for colour, silhouettes, statuary, and the sort of eclectic mix he calls "courtyard cozy," all combined to produce a balanced composition.

Left: *Plumeria and Bougainvillea, both able to thrive under dry conditions, create a tunnel of loveliness between two vast site huts. This coastal part, the area Wijaya calls the foreshore parklands, gives over to a more gentle landscape treatment in homage to a Sydney cliff walk.*

Above: *The main pool terrace, also a restaurant and bar, surveys stunning views of Jimbaran Bay. Clumps of Plumeria and crimson Bougainvillea provide puddles of shade.*

Right: *The plunge pools in each villa are shaded from the village lanes by clever border planting utilizing flowering shrubs and local cactus.*

Opposite: *The resort's main pool is connected to the lower jungle pools and spas by a dramatically architectural waterfall, part of a large curtain wall of limestone now covered by by Wijaya's artistically natural planting.*

Above: *A view of the main reception building, a traditional tiered building called a* wantilan.

Right: *The main dining room, called Taman Wantilan, is more water garden than restaurant. Classical Balinese spouts, from a North Balinese temple, eject water from islands planted with Cocothrinax readii and Plumeria rubra.*

Far Left, above and below: *Stark Plumeria silhouettes provide relief from the relentless blue sky at the hotel.*

Left: *Native trees shade a thatched-roof pavilion modelled on Samoan meeting huts. The views overlooking Jimbaran Bay are sensational. The palm-like plant on the right is a Pandanus, which grows extensively along the coast.*

Below: *Bougainvillea, Russellia equisetiformis and Pandanus, all suited to dry conditions, are among the plants along a flight of steps leading to one of the resort's seven private beaches.*

Gardens in Nusa Dua

Nusa Dua lies on the Bukit Peninsula near Bali's southernmost tip, fringed by a sweeping beach of uncommon beauty along the blue waters of the Badung Strait. Tanjung Benoa, the point north of Nusa Dua, was once an important trading port; a Chinese temple stands as a reminder of its busy past, although most of the merchants left its shores long ago for more prosperous Denpasar. Near Nusa Dua itself, the small village of Bualu once had its noble houses and there were, as everywhere, temples and shrines. But this is the driest part of Bali; lack of rain and thin, sandy soil rendered the area unsuitable for rice farming and until a decade or so ago, its sparse population derived a livelihood mostly from fishing and harvesting the coconut palms that grew extensively on the peninsula.

The Nusa Dua Concept

All these factors played a part in the selection of Nusa Dua as the place to introduce a new and novel concept, one prompted by the remarkable rise in tourism in Southeast Asia and the Pacific and a concern over its future effects. Accounting for a mere one per cent of international tourist arrivals in 1960, the region had three per cent by 1970, seven per cent by 1980 and over eleven per cent by 1989. The impact of such an increase was considerable, culturally as well as economically, leading to many studies on how best to absorb the growing number of visitors while also preserving those qualities that attracted them.

Viewing its own future, the Indonesian government decided that one answer lay in the creation of integrated resorts carefully designed not only to meet the demands of discriminating visitors for security, comfort, and easy access but also to have a minimal effect on the environment and traditional culture. Only by taking such a step, it was felt, could the inevitable expansion of tourism be to some extent guided and the national heritage protected.

Left: A corner of the verandah off the Grand Hyatt's main lobby, looking towards the beach.
Right Top: A wedding procession pauses in a corner of a beach-side garden at Nusa Dua, on Bali's Bukit Peninsula.
Right Below: The shallow reef off Nusa Dua beach harbours interesting life forms which can be inspected at low tide.

Bali, undoubtedly the country's most legendary attraction, was a natural place to start translating the concept into reality.

With help from the World Bank, work began in 1969 on a master plan, completed in 1971; two years later, the Bali Tourism Development Corporation was formed as a state–owned company to oversee the project and be responsible for such infrastructure features as roads, water, electricity and sewage treatment. The plan called for the development of a site at Nusa Dua covering 310 hectares, including a beach front of 3.5 kilometres, with a further 115 hectares reserved for future expansion.

A design committee consisting of architects and hotel development experts laid down strict rules for the complex. All buildings, for example, would be limited to a height of 15 metres or about that of a coconut palm and would project a Balinese character. Landscape and open spaces would be predominant and oriented towards pedestrians; the removal of large trees was prohibited except by permit for construction purposes and the public was guaranteed use of all areas within 30 metres of the shoreline. Even Balinese cosmic notions of orientation were taken into account, with the sacred direction facing Gunung Agung (*kaja*) being the area in which the shrines of the hotels were to be located, while the impure *kelod* or seaward direction was to be the location for the least sacred of a hotel's activities (in the case of one hotel, their discotheque was assigned to this location).

Settlers in the designated area, some 170 families, were relocated to the vicinity of Bualu and given assistance in obtaining jobs and, for their children, priority status in a planned hotel school. Fishermen who had used the beaches were also given an opportunity to supply various kinds of boats to tourists. Work then began on roads, water pipes, a telecommunications system, and landscaping of the common areas.

Translation Into Reality

The first facility, the Bualu Hotel, opened in 1978 and initially served as a training centre for hotel workers under the supervision of the Directorate General of Tourism with the cooperation of the United Nations Development Programme and the International Labour Organisation. Nearly all the first group of 120 students came from the Nusa Dua area. Now operated on a commercial basis, the Bualu has been joined by eight other hotels, all

Opposite: The golf course at Nusa Dua, where remaining trees from the original grove of coconut palms create a unique hazard for golfers.

Above: The stone fountain at the entrance to the Nusa Dua complex; although the material is traditional, this candi dwara pala pada *is a more modern version of traditional Balinese temple structures.*

in the five-star category and offering a combined total of more than 3,500 guest rooms. The integrated resort concept itself, drawing on the Nusa Dua experience, is now being applied as a basic policy in other parts of Indonesia, from Baturaden in the mountains of Central Java to the Indian Ocean island of Nias off the west coast of Sumatra.

Today, less than 20 years after it opened, the Nusa Dua complex seems a long-established part of the landscape, though a very different one from the bare, sandy expanses where mostly coconuts grew in the past. At the entrance to the resort stands an imposing *candi bentar*, a split stone gate resembling a tower divided into two parts and also common to Balinese temples, while nearby is a more modern-style fountain gate, also made of stone, called a *candi dwara pala pada*; this is surmounted by a fearsome head of Kala, the underworld god.

Within the gates lies a seductive world, one of meticulously tended lawns, shady trees and massed beds of flowering plants; winding pathways are ideal for a relaxing stroll, ponds are filled with aquatic plants and pools are reminiscent of the gardens of traditional Balinese palaces. The tiled and thatched rooftops of various properties are glimpsed only occasionally through the pervading greenery.

For all its park-like atmosphere, however, the magical sense of Bali is strongly present. In a convenient, village-like setting, there are shops selling the best of local crafts, restaurants and an amphitheatre for cultural performances. Old temples have also been preserved; one in the heart of the Grand Hyatt resort is still visited by high priests who come to make offerings and conduct ceremonies; its architecture served as inspiration for the nearby Pasar Senggol, where Balinese dances are staged.

Following the general guidelines, each of the Nusa Dua hotels has created a distinctive ambiance. One of the most notable can be found within the grounds of the Grand Hyatt Bali, an extensive complex that opened in mid-1991 and that quickly became renowned for its comforts and the beauty of its gardens.

Below: The fountain gateway at the entrance of the Nusa Dua Beach Hotel, one of the earliest hotels to open, has become a well known landmark.

Above: *An avenue of Delonix regia trees in Nusa Dua. Throughout the complex, buildings are low rise, often shaded by tall trees.*

Left: *Bougainvillea and yellow bamboo at the entrance of the Grand Hyatt.*

Overleaf: *Private swimming pool, surrounded by a luxuriant garden, at one of the Wantalan Golf Villas, part of the Bali Golf and Country Club at Nusa Dua. Inaugurated in 1991, the club's course was designed by Robin Nelson and Rodney Wright and voted "one of Asia's five best golf courses" by experts in Fortune magazine. Each of the spacious, Balinese-style villas offers privacy and tranquility in a secluded enclave, with self-contained bedrooms, sitting areas, open-air gazebos and pools.*

The Amanusa Garden

Amanresorts is a chain of luxury facilities in some of the world's most romantic places, internationally renowned for their imaginative architecture and sensitive use of beautiful natural sites. Amanusa, the newest of three Aman properties in Bali, is strikingly located atop a hill overlooking the Nusa Dua area, surrounded by the Bali Golf and Country Club.

An airy openness characterizes the resort's 35 free-standing villas, each with its own private Balinese-style courtyard; eight have private swimming pools as well and extended areas for entertainment. Guests can choose views of the golf course, the Nusa Dua peninsula, or the Indian Ocean. Other facilities include an open, pavilion-style lobby, two restaurants offering continental and Asian specialties, a bar, library, and antique shop, tennis courts, and a beach club on a white-sand beach protected by an off-shore reef that forms a sheltered lagoon.

Most Aman resorts have rather spare gardens, making use of natural contours and specimens already growing on the site. At Amanusa, existing vegetation has been retained around the villas, which means that most of the garden areas consist of indigenous plants resistant to the dry conditions that prevail in Nusa Dua. Introduced species–Plumeria, Bougainvillea, Allamanda, and a few palms near the entrance–similarly thrive in such places but add colour to the landscape. In contrast to the luxuriant, jungle-like gardens seen elsewhere in Bali, a simple, open scheme is preferred here, one that admirably suits the location.

Left: *A long pergola covered with flowering creepers provides shade beside the main swimming pool; Nusa Dua bay can be seen in the background.*

Top: *A terraced area, alternating stepping stones and low foliage, shaded by native trees and white-flowering Plumeria; this is a landscaping device pioneered by Geoffrey Bawa of Sri Lanka.*

Right: *The main building of the Amanusa, overlooking Nusa Dua; Bougainvillea and Plumeria are planted below, offering both colour and fragrance.*

Opposite Top: *From most of the resort's balconies one has a distant view of the sea. Set amidst the existing vegetation of Euphorbia, Agave, Pandanus and Kapok trees are additional plantings of Rhoeo interspersed with* Adenium obesum, *a plant that thrives in dry, sandy soil. Yellow Bamboo acts as a screen for extra privacy between the cottages.*

Opposite Bottom: *The entrance to the resort. The palms in the foreground are Bismarkia nobilis. Originally from Madagascar, this is an impressive species with grey-green leaves that can measure several metres across.*

The Grand Hyatt Garden

Prior to the opening of the Grand Hyatt lay years of careful planning, not only for the buildings that drew on traditional Balinese architectural concepts but also for the 40 acres of tropical plants that provide a setting for them. The landscape design was the work of Tong, Clark, and McCelvey, a Honolulu firm with wide resort experience, executed on site by Indo Sekar of Bali. It called for thousands of plants, ranging from trees and shrubs to grass lawns and water lilies, and demanded considerable skill at overcoming a number of horticultural challenges.

The basic scheme was inspired by Bali's legendary water palaces with their numerous moats, pools, fountains and cascades that delight the eye through a sequence of courtyards. The huge size of the Nusa Dua garden offered an opportunity for other landscapes as well; some of these, especially on the long beach front, presented certain problems.

The foremost difficulty was the local soil, which was mostly sand and offered little nourishment for decorative shrubs and trees. Indeed, the soil layer was thinner at the Grand Hyatt site than elsewhere on Nusa Dua and thus required particular care in both treatment and plant selection. Added difficulties are the lack of rainfall and seasonal sea winds that wreak havoc on delicate shrubs subjected to their full force. Considerable care was required in the selection of the larger shrubs and trees that were to act as screening from the wind. An obvious solution was to look for plants with a proven ability not only to survive but to flourish under precisely these conditions, and the search yielded many specimens that in terms of beauty as well as stamina, are well suited to garden use.

Plants for Seaside Gardens

One example, which can be seen in several parts of the garden, is the so-called Sea Hibiscus. This actually occurs in two forms with separate botanical names, *Hibiscus tiliaceus* and *Thespesia populnea*. Both belong to the Hibiscus family, are native to the tropical Orient and Pacific region and have similar leathery round or heart-shaped leaves and five-petaled yellow flowers that turn a

Left: *Night-blooming water lilies add their beauty to the Grand Hyatt lobby pool during the soft tropical evenings.*

Top: *A detail of one of the water gardens at the Grand Hyatt. The mass of cerise and white Bougainvillea seems to crowd almost into the water itself.*
Above: *A contrast to the terraced waterways above, this limpid pond is home to water lilies.*
Right: *The large pool just off the lobby of the Grand Hyatt is fringed by showy beds of Bougainvillea, with yellow and orange-leaf Crotons in the foreground; at the right-hand corner can be seen the orange petals of an Ixora.*

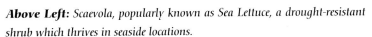

Above Left: *Scaevola, popularly known as Sea Lettuce, a drought-resistant shrub which thrives in seaside locations.*

Above Right: *Coccoloba uvifera, the Sea Grape; the fruit is used in some places for jelly, while the platter-like leaves make the small tree an attractive addition to any garden.*

Opposite Top Left: *A species of Pandan, commonly called the Seashore Screwpine; the pineapple-like fruits are edible after cooking.*

Opposite Top Centre: *Calotropis gigantea, called the Crown Flower in some countries; the flowers are used in Balinese ceremonies.*

Opposite Top Right: *Pseuderanthemum reticulatum, a native Pacific shrub which is frequently used in the Grand Hyatt gardens.*

Opposite Below: *Colour contrasts are provided through massed plantings of various shrubs; among those shown here are variegated Pedilanthus, Pseudaranthemum (the Golden Eranthemum), Acalypha and Scaevola.*

darker hue before they fall. The more common of the two is *H. tiliaceus*, closer botanically to the familiar Hibiscus shrub. It tends to grow near the ground in a twisting shape, though mature specimens can become quite large and have trunks half a metre or more in diameter. *Thespesia populnea* is much more of a proper, upright tree, often reaching a considerable height and providing welcome shade along pathways. The Balinese call it *waru lot* and once used its almost flavourless wood to make food containers.

Another handsome specimen well-adapted to seaside gardens is *Calotropis gigantea*, called *manori* or *manduri* in Bali and elsewhere the crown flower. A member of the milkweed family, this large shrub has thick, greyish-green leaves, a milky sap and white or lavender-coloured flowers with five twisted, starlike petals and an elegant "crown" of stamens rising from the middle. Scaevola, also a familiar beach shrub throughout the region, proved invaluable where massed greenery was needed on pathways and ponds near the sea. Commonly known as the Sea Lettuce tree, this has pale-coloured, fleshy leaves and is able to withstand even strong, salty winds without becoming unsightly; the five-lobed flower occurs on only one side of the corolla tube, giving rise to another popular name, the "half-flower".

Equally useful in such locations is a variety of Pandanus, the Seashore Screwpine, which resembles a palm with aerial roots serving as braces and clusters of spiny leaves at the end of branches. There are male and female trees; the latter produces a pineapple-like fruit that turns deep yellow as it ripens.

One of the most usual small trees in this part of the garden is *Coccoloba uvifera*, the Sea Grape, which periodically displays long clusters of small round fruit that can be used to make jelly. The stiff, rounded, platter–like leaves, shading from yellowish to olive–green with prominent veins, also assist in making this an attractive addition to the landscape plan.

Other drought–resistant specimens include *Terminalia catappa*, the Sea Almond, a native of the Indo–Pacific region whose branches spread in layers; *Calophyllum inophyllum*, with tough, glossy leaves, small fragrant flowers and round fruit from which lamp oil can be extracted; and, of course, the ubiquitous coconut palm, *Cocos nucifera*, some of which remain from the vast plantations that once covered Nusa Dua.

A Variety of Vistas

Away from the sea, along walkways linking the resort's various areas where sun and shade alternate, additions of rich soil and other nutrients have made it possible to create constantly changing vistas both colourful and luxuriant.

A major source of colour is Bougainvillea, seen spilling over walls and the banks of ponds in many parts of the garden. This hardy creeper whose brilliant "flowers" are actually coloured bracts is named after Louis de Bougainville, a French navigator who came across it in Rio de Janiero in the 18th century; it quickly spread through the tropical and sub–tropical world and countless hybrids can now be seen in almost every hue.

Quite a few of the Grand Hyatt garden's other decorative shrubs and trees also originated outside the island but have become such a part of the local scene they are now regarded as virtual natives. The fragrant Plumeria is a native of the New World and arrived in Asia with the first Europeans. *Delonix regia*, variously known as the Flame Tree, the Flamboyant and the Royal Poinciana and now common to every warm country, was first seen in Madagascar, as was *Ravenala madagascariensis*, the Traveller's Palm, virtually a symbol of tropical luxuriance. *Bauhinia purpurea*, the Orchid Tree, with its elegant purple blossoms, had a relatively short distance to travel from its native India, but *Spathodea campanulata*, the African Tulip Tree, came all the way from Uganda.

Opposite Top and Below: *The seaside villas of the Grand Hyatt enjoy their own ponds, where white ducks can sometimes be seen; some of the villas have enclosed gardens with traditional Balinese gateways.*

Above: *A seaside villa, with its walls ensuring total privacy. The pool in front is surrounded by Bougainvillea and Crotons.*

Shrubs have been chosen both for their flowers and their ornamental foliage. *Pseuderanthemum reticulatum*, a Pacific native
sometimes called the Golden Eranthemum, is widely used in
massed plantings. Similarly reliable are Codiaeums, which come
in a jewel–like assortment of reds, golds, and oranges; Ixora, with
frequent clusters of scarlet blossoms; sky–blue Plumbago; red
Hibiscus and Allamanda, the Golden Trumpet.

In some of the courtyard plantings can be seen the Sumatran
Banana (*Musa sumatrana*), grown for its beautifully patterned
leaves. The Heliconia is another member of the same family, represented here by several varieties that range from low–growing
clumps to the giant red–flowering *H. caribaea*, one of the most
striking of all tropical exotics. Bamboo is as basic to Balinese life
as the coconut palm and appears not only in the customary
green but also in pure gold, yellow with bold green stripes and a
dark, unusual shade that is almost black. Amidst the plantings
there are assorted ground covers and other low–growing plants
like spiky, green–and–purple Rhoeo, yellow–flowering Wedelia,
variegated, grass–like Chlorophytum and ferns of various kinds.

*Above: Entrance to the Watercourt Restaurant, with contemporary carvings
and a glimpse of the pool beyond.*
*Right: Water cascades over a series of levels in the Watercourt restaurant,
planted with ferns, Aroids, Bougainvillea, Plumeria and palms to increase the
cooling effect.*

Above: This assortment of water plants includes the sacred pink Lotus, Water Lilies and tall Typha angustifolia. The Water Lily seen in close-up, is found in both day and night-blooming varieties.

Right: There are three different groups of Water Lily in the Grand Hyatt's garden; this white-flowered variety is Nymphaea lotus.

Below: Nelumbo nucifera, *the lotus, regarded as sacred by both Hindus and Buddhists.*

Bottom: Bauhinia purpurea, *commonly called the Orchid Tree because of its elegantly shaped flowers.*

Overleaf: *The pool in front of the Grand Hyatt's Chinese restaurant, where the striking green-tiled roof contrasts with the orange tiles covering the rest of the resort's buildings.*

The Water Theme

Water is the dominant theme of the Grand Hyatt landscape. Vast ponds on either side of the open entrance lobby, their banks a blaze of ever-blooming Bougainvillea, make a dramatic statement for new arrivals. These ponds offer a varied display of Nymphaea or water lilies, both day and night-blooming, and lead to an interlinking system of smaller ponds, waterfalls and streams. Elsewhere, picturesque lagoons lap just below the balconies of the ground floor guest rooms, where friendly ducks as well as fish have learned to gather for leftovers at breakfast time.

At the Watercourt Restaurant, fountains gush from stone carvings into a reflecting pool and one outdoor area is sheltered by a venerable *Waringin*. The Nelayan Seafood Restaurant also overlooks water, in this case a pond from which the elegant leaves and flowers of the sacred lotus rise, while the Balinese Feature Pool, adorned with traditional statues, cascades over three different levels to provide a constant background of soothing sound.

In addition, extending the theme into recreation, the resort offers a wide choice of swimming facilities, among them a 120-metre free-form pool, a 50-metre water slide leading to a river pool, a lap pool at the sports centre and a private pool for guests at the exclusive Regency Club.

Also planted extensively at the resort is the celebrated *Nelumbo nucifera*, the sacred lotus, a religious emblem throughout Asia. Although very different in their growing habits–lotus leaves and flowers rise high above the water while those of lilies remain on the surface–the two have often been confused. Other water plants seen at the Grand Hyatt include the slender *Typha angustifolia*, which resembles the Bulrush and *Cyperus alternifolius*, the so-called "umbrella plant" and a relative of the Papyrus.

A Creation Still Evolving

Even by tropical standards, the landscape of the Grand Hyatt is still youthful. Over the coming years the sea-front trees will form a protective screen, and the courtyards will become even more luxuriant. Present-day vistas will alter through growth and through the addition of new specimens. Whatever changes take place, however, it will continue to be one of Bali's most imaginative horticultural creations. It is truly a worthy companion to the famous Bali Hyatt garden at Sanur.

The Novotel Benoa Garden

Overlooking Tanjung Benoa Beach at Nusa Dua, the Novotel Benoa is built in the style of a Balinese village with traditional thatched-roof buildings and courtyards. The resort was in a state of considerable disrepair when architect Lek Bunnag and landscape designer Bill Bensley were commissioned to renovate both structures and gardens, a task they completed in the remarkably short time of less than a year.

A large open-sided lobby pavilion provides the central feature, while pathways lead to 180 guest rooms, each with either a balcony or a private garden, and twelve beach cabanas. Facilities include three swimming pools, Asian and Western restaurants, tennis courts, a fully-equipped fitness centre, and an outdoor stage for cultural performances. The steep thatched roofs of many of the buildings were inspired by rice granaries from the island of Lombok, while native coral stone has been used for walls and gateways to enhance the rustic, natural appearance.

Bill Bensley's landscape is designed to blend harmoniously with the architecture, using graceful coconut palms and drought-resistant ornamentals to achieve varied colours, predominantly yellow and white, and textures in this arid part of Bali. The village-like arrangement allows a series of changing vistas as one procedes through gateways to the different courtyards. Each of the seafront cabanas has its own sunning garden and Balinese-style outdoor bathroom. As in many of the gardens he has created throughout the tropical world, Bensley utililizes numerous works of art, some traditional and some whimsical. A statue of a reclining woman in traditional dress, for example, lounges seductively beside a sunken lap pool, while the Crocokiss Bar has reptilian details.

Opposite: *A stone reclining woman beside a lap pool at the Novotel Benoa; coconut palms rise against the sky.*
Right: *Bougainvillea and Hibiscus bloom on the left, while on the right is a Plumeria tree; the gate is a contemporary adaptation of a traditional style.*

Top: *A thatched-roof lumbung, or rice granary, on a wall; the flowering creeper at the top is Bougainvillea.*

Right: *A variegated form of Polycias grows along one of the pathways, while the large water jars, statuary and thatched roofs add to the Balinese atmosphere of the resort.*

Opposite Top: *Yellow bamboo cascades over one of the many interconnecting pathways in the grounds.*

Opposite Below: Arundodonax versicolor, *popularly called white bamboo, grows beside a doorway.*

Gardens in Ubud

More perhaps than any other place, Ubud was the inspiration half a century ago for Miguel Covarrubias' famous observation that "everybody in Bali seems to be an artist". Today, Ubud and its neighbouring villages still project a palpable sense of creativity. Painters, weavers and wood-carvers can be seen working in studios, shops displaying their creations line the narrow roads and the sound of *gamelan* orchestras announces almost daily performances of Balinese dance and temple festivals. All this attracted a cosmopolitan group of art-loving expatriates to settle in the area during the 1930s, and to produce most of the books, films, photographs and anthropological studies that made Bali internationally famous.

But now, as in the past, Ubud's appeal is based on more than artistic fervour. Its natural setting in the hills is spectacularly beautiful with dramatic ravines, winding rivers and streams, the most scenic of the island's famous terraced rice fields, refreshing waterfalls and sacred pools, even a primeval forest full of monkeys. It is easy to see why many Bali-lovers of the present have also chosen to make their homes in the region, creating a number of notable contemporary gardens.

A Centre of the Arts

Part of the kingdom of Gianyar, Ubud had a rich cultural tradition in pre-colonial days. It was a seat of *punggawa* or feudal lords who paid allegiance to the Gianyar *raja*, and also a famous source of traditional medicine. The name of the village, in fact, comes from *ubad*, the Balinese word for medicine. Its larger fame, though, began with the arrival of a young German aristocrat in the late 1920s.

Walter Spies was the son of a diplomat and had already experienced a colourful youth in Czarist Russia, Germany and Holland before boarding a ship for Java at the age of 28. There he lived for several years in the palace of the Sultan of Yogyakarta, directing a European orchestra and also painting. A visit to Bali in 1925 was the beginning of a life-long love affair with the island. He moved to Ubud in 1927, staying first in the palace of the ruling Sukawati family and then building his own thatched bamboo house and studio on the side of a ravine at Campuan, "Where Two Rivers Meet," a place of great spiritual significance.

Opposite: *The lush garden and house of artist Walter Spies, who lived in Ubud during the 1930s, is now part of the Hotel Campuan near Ubud.*
Above: *A painting by Walter Spies, who introduced new techniques to Balinese painting (courtesy Walter Spies Foundation).*

Interested in every aspect of Balinese culture–not only its painting but also its dance, music, religion, black magic, and everyday life–Spies became a central source of information for other talented Westerners lured by Bali's legendary image. Miguel and Rose Covarrubias drew on his knowledge for their still widely read work on the island, as did Margaret Mead and her husband Gregory Bateson for their pioneering anthropological studies and Colin McPhee for his research into Balinese music. Spies advised on a number of films and for one of them, choreographed the exciting *kecak* dance with the assistance of the dancer–ethnologist Katharane Mershon. With the Dutch painter Rudolf Bonnet, he exerted a powerful influence over Balinese painting, leading it away from static, traditional forms into the treatment of new subject matter and the use of new techniques. Most of all, perhaps, he painted himself, not in great quantity but with a haunting, almost surrealistic touch that made his works famous among distinguished visitors.

Spies was arrested on a morals charge at the end of 1938. Released after eight months–during which his *gamelan* orchestra came to Denpasar to play outside the wall of his prison–he was interned when Germany invaded Holland in 1940. Two years later, he was drowned when a Japanese torpedo bomber sank the ship that was carrying him and other prisoners of war to Ceylon.

Ubud's moment of international renown had ended, but it was to flower again, almost as vividly, with the arrival of another group of talented residents who have found their own versions of paradise amid its natural beauties and cultural stimulation.

Blending Old and New

Several of Ubud's notable landscapes today are a blend of past and present. For example, the ornately carved Puri Saraswati, a former royal residence, has become the spectacular backdrop for the Lotus Café, featuring a lotus pond originally planted by the noted photographer Rio Helmi and a garden developed by Rodolfo Giusti, present owner of the popular café.

Spies' simple house at Campuan, overlooking the picturesque River Oos just a kilometer northwest of Ubud, has been renovated but still stands as part of a bungalow complex. Shrines, statues and Balinese-style ponds enhance the luxuriant garden, the sound of water flowing down from one level to another cre-

Above: *A view of the pond of Cafe Lotus in front of Ubud's Puri Saraswati.*
Left: *Many scenes of Ubud's luxuriant landscapes are captured in paintings displayed within the Museum Puri Lukisan, seen here behind its water garden.*
Opposite Top and Below: *The path following the edge of a ravine and the shrine shaded by the inevitable Banyan or Waringin tree are in the gardens of the house once belonging to Walter Spies.*

Above: *The jungle-like planting in the garden of Cody and Lyn Shwaiko, a part of the Puri Saren complex in Ubud.*
Opposite: *Orchids, Maidenhair and Bird's Nest Ferns, Calathea and Cordylines fill the garden, with Heliconia rostrata providing a splash of colour.*

Above and opposite: The unique home of interior designer Linda Garland, in Nyuh Kuning near Ubud.

ates a soothing atmosphere and a modern guest can enjoy the same breathtaking views that Spies and his guests once did.

The Puri Lukisan, "Palace of Paintings", is Ubud's leading art museum, founded in 1956 by Rudolf Bonnet and Cokorda Gede Agung Sukawati, the local prince who befriended Walter Spies and other artistic residents of the 30s. The garden here contains numerous sculptures treating traditional subjects in modern style, while the museum itself displays a comprehensive collection of the naturalistic art encouraged by Bonnet and Spies.

Contemporary Landscapes

Completely new gardens in the Ubud area have been created by a later generation of painters, designers, film-makers or simply escapists entranced by Bali. These range from small compounds with comparatively limited plant material–although carefully chosen and placed–to extensive landscapes covering several acres and often a number of levels.

One of the most celebrated current residents is Linda Garland, whose impact on Balinese arts and crafts has been profound. After inspiring a whole new industry of decorative painted woodcarvings now exported throughout the world, Garland moved on to interior design and filled countless famous houses–including one belonging to the singer David Bowie–with her signature furniture made of giant bamboo. Now the versatile bamboo, of which 150 species are found in Indonesia alone, has become a passionate cause that occupies most of her time. In

Top: *Buildings made of bamboo and thatched with* alang alang *grass in part of the compound created by Linda Garland.*
Above: *The split bamboo floor of the verandah juts out into the ravine, making the house like an extension of the garden.*
Opposite: *Another Ubud house which flows into the garden is that of Lorne Blair; the room in the foreground has no rail to mark the edge of the floor.*

1993, she founded the Environmental Bamboo Foundation to stimulate research into the plant and its environmental value as well as its uses as a substitute for wood in an age of fast-diminishing forests.

Headquarters for the foundation are Linda Garland's home at Nyuh Kuning ("Yellow Coconut Village"), a unique collection of structures so distinctive they have been featured in *Architectural Digest*. Here Garland subtly shaped the landscape so that it extends as a series of rolling plains on several levels to a river below and merges naturally into neighbouring terraced rice fields. Like her current interests, the garden owes more to practical considerations than to the purely ornamental; every plant in it serves a useful function, even the attractive foliage Heliconias, the red leaves of which serve as unusual plates at dinner parties.

Also in Nyuh Kuning is the home of writer and film-maker Lorne Blair, whose BBC documentary about Indonesia, *Ring of Fire*, won a wide audience. Blair's house, consisting of various parts of a central Javanese dwelling, is open on all sides and thus offers unobstructed views of a garden designed by a resident painter, Dewa Putralaya, as well as of rice fields and a volcano beyond.

Ian Van Werringan, a painter, has built a multi-level house on the picturesque Sayan ridge. The house overlooks the Ayung River, which is popular with white-water rafting enthusiasts. Here the garden effect is one of an only slightly tamed jungle, a dense planting of ornamental and native specimens decorated with primitive sculptures.

Other gardens of charm and distinction are constantly being added to the Ubud landscape, some in secluded private compounds and therefore unseen by the casual visitor, others in larger bungalow complexes. Though often less "traditional" than the older ones, many display a similar artistic flair, using boldly coloured foliage plants in a limited area to create striking patterns. In one of the most spectacular, located on the slope of a valley, brilliant red Cordylines and yellow Codiaeums stand out in contrast to a neatly trimmed lawn, making a modernistic yet harmonious statement against the lush jungle-like background. Another, a spacious private estate north of Ubud, has followed the contours of the Sayan ridge in a series of wonderfully lush terraces that artfully blends native plants with introduced species so that it is difficult for a layman to distinguish between them.

Right: *A jewel-like swath of neatly-trimmed lawn forms a focal point for this Ubud garden in a secluded valley. Palms of varying heights contribute to the atmosphere, while colour is provided by Heliconias and foliage plants; on the left an Anthurium displays its bold inflorescences.*

Above: *A footpath of volcanic stone winds between colourful Cordylines and Codiaeums in the same garden.*

Bali Bird Park

Created by its directors Edi Swaboda and I Putu Gede Sidartha, the Bali Bird Park in Singapadu was formerly an area of terraced rice fields. Today it is home to over 1,000 birds housed in some 60 different aviaries, set in a lush planting of more than 300 exotic trees and other specimens. Peacocks, parrots, cockatoos, macaws, and scarlet ibis are among the birds on display. The extensive gardens contain a particularly large collection of palms, ranging from the familiar coconut to rare varieties, as well as cacti and other drought–loving plants. Dominating the park is a dramatic Troraja which was dismantled and moved to the site.

Above Left: One of the many palms that have been planted in the park.
Above Middle: The Foxtail Palm (Wodyetia bifurca).
Above Right: The Bottle Palm is set in front of a lake planted with water lilies.
Right: The Triangle Palm (Dypsis decaryi).
Opposite: A planting near the entrance of the park, with various palms, cycads, and cacti.
Overleaf: Details of some of the plants and landscapes found around Ubud, where the altitude, rivers and springs combine to produce an enviable lushness to the vegetation.

Four Seasons Resort Bali at Sayan

The Sayan Ridge, west of Ubud, is one of Bali's most famous beauty spots, offering memorable views of rice terraces dropping down to the Ayung River. This dramatic landscape has been incorporated into the design of Four Seasons Resort Bali at Sayan, which sought to merge natural features and buildings as seamlessly as possible.

The brief given to British architect John Heah called for all existing rice fields, vegetable gardens, and trees to be retained and for buildings to "either blend or disappear into the landscape." The result was eighteen sunken villas with lily ponds on the roofs, assorted water features, and rustic landscaping that takes full advantage of the celebrated terrain. Walking around the resort, guests not only see working rice fields in all their seasonal variations of colour but also such kitchen plants as lemon grass, chili peppers, and tapioca with its handsome, hand-shaped leaves; traditional forms of irrigation employing a complex system of bamboo tubes are also integrated into the garden design.

A 55-metre-long teak and steel footbridge at tree-top level leads to a large lotus pond, then via a staircase into the main building where the panoramic views are as theatrical as the innovative entrance. Suspended teak walkways lead to 18 terrace suites, while other facilities include a paddy-shaped swimming pool overlooking the Ayung River on two levels, restaurants, a bar, and an extensive health club and spa overlooking the valley. Interiors, also designed by Heah's company, display many Balinese features and materials.

Cascading water features create a soothing atmosphere in the central building, which is also planted with a luxuriant assortment of stag-horn ferns, climbing Thunbergia, Heliconias, and Banyan trees to define different areas and frame vistas into the surrounding landscape.

Left: *A rooftop lotus pond, planted with lotus and other water plants, helps the construction to blend into the landscape.*

Top: *The central building at the resort, surrounded by spectacular views of the Sayan countryside*

Above: *A rooftop lotus pool, with contours that follow those of the famous rice terraces, blends almost seamlessly into the landscape.*

Left and Opposite: *Coconut palms and water features are components of the rustic landscaping that make the resort seem part of its natural setting.*

Begawan Giri Estate

On the Sayan ridge, north of Ubud, lies the small village of Begawan, famous for three nearby holy springs. One of these, known as Toya Mampeh, is believed to have magical powers for cleansing the heart and mind and curing various illnesses. It is now located within the premises of what is almost certainly one of the great landscaped gardens, not just of the Ubud area but of Bali as whole. Called Begawan Giri Estate, this began as a private holiday home and has grown into a exclusive private resort that has five villa complexes, each a self-contained world of luxury, as well as an outstanding spa, an amphitheatre for traditional dance performances and wonderful food and beverage outlets. The architect of the project was Cheong Yew Kuan, while Karl Princic, and later John Pettigrew, assisted in designing the extensive landscape. The guiding vision, however, was provided by Bradley and Debora Gardner, the owners. Over the past ten years, they have spent long periods on the site studying its natural contours, researching its history and personally transforming it into what is already a creation of exceptional beauty and botanical interest.

Nearly 2500 trees have been planted, among them such useful specimens as teak, mahogany, tamarind, avocado, mango, mangosteen, durian, breadfruit, *rambutan* and coconut. There are also flowering trees like the Flamboyant, the African Tulip and the fragrant Champaca. Spring–fed ponds are stocked with a reliable source of freshwater fish and vegetable gardens are tended by kitchen staff. In addition, numerous exotic ornamentals including Heliconias, Gingers, Hibiscus, Ixora, Anthuriums and orchids have been incorporated into the environment.

The most impressive part of the garden is to be found on the slopes of the ravine leading down to the river, where along flights of stone steps and around terraces, some memorable tropical effects have been achieved. From tall Heliconias with huge paddle–shaped leaves, long pinkish–orange bracts hang like chandeliers amid the greenery; maidenhair ferns droop languidly over mossy walls; Cordylines provide sudden splashes of colour; and *Phalaenopsis*, the moon orchid, appears to grow wild on tree trunks.

Left: *A natural spring flows through the gardens at Begawan Giri Estate. Cascading down the hillside it is reputed to have healing powers.*
Right: *One of the five palatial residences, 'Wanakasa" or "Forest in the Mist", is essentially a treehouse built on stilts rising from the surrounding vegetation.*

Left, Below and Overleaf: *Fresh water from the spring on the site of Begawan Giri is used to fill the estate's spa pools, all of which have a natural "Garden of Eden" appearance.*